Social Care in a
Mixed Economy

Public Policy and Management

Series Editor: Professor R.A.W. Rhodes, Department of Politics, University of York.

The effectiveness of public policies is a matter of public concern and the efficiency with which policies are put into practice is a continuing problem for governments of all political persuasions. This series contributes to these debates by publishing informed, in-depth and contemporary analyses of public administration, public policy and public management.

The intention is to go beyond the usual textbook approach to the analysis of public policy and management and to encourage authors to move debate about their issue forward. In this sense, each book both describes current thinking and research, and explores future policy directions. Accessibility is a key feature and, as a result, the series will appeal to academics and their students as well as to the informed practitioner.

Current Titles Include:

Social Care in a Mixed Economy

Gerald Wistow, Martin Knapp,
Brian Hardy and Caroline Allen

Open University Press
Buckingham • Philadelphia

Open University Press
Celtic Court
22 Ballmoor
Buckingham
MK18 1XW

and
1900 Frost Road, Suite 101
Bristol, PA 19007, USA

First Published 1994
Reprinted 1995

© Crown Copyright 1994

A catalogue record of this book is available from the British Library

Library of Congress Cataloging-in-Publication Data

Wistow, Gerald
    Social care in a mixed economy/
  Gerald Wistow, Martin Knapp, Brian Hardy, and Caroline Allen.
      p.   cm — (Public policy and management series)
  Includes bibliographical references and index.
  ISBN 0-335-19044-8   0-335-19043-X (pbk)
    1. Social service—Government policy—Great Britain.   2. Mixed
economy—Great Britain.   3. Great Britain—Economic conditions—1945
I. Wistow, Gerald, 1946– . II. Series
HV248.S62 1994
361.941–dc20   93–32694
                                                              CIP

Typeset by Jane Dennett at the PSSRU, University of Kent at Canterbury
Printed in Great Britain by St Edmundsbury Press Ltd, Bury St Edmunds, Suffolk

Contents

List of tables, boxes and figures

Boxes

Figures

Preface

April 1993 saw the implementation of a major policy initiative in the field of community care. The associated legislative changes are designed to transform not only the role of local authority social services departments, but also, in the process, the lives of some of the most vulnerable people in the community. These changes reflect the broader introduction of competitive forces into the public sector and the more specific focus on 'enabling, not providing' as the principal role of local government.

In their detailed form, the community care arrangements mirror many aspects of the National Health Service market for which the Department of Health was also responsible. However, the community care changes may also be seen to be more radical and far-reaching than the NHS reforms. In particular, the social care market is to be an external market, rather than an internal one, in which independent sector providers are to play a substantial part.

This book is based upon a study of how twenty-five local authorities were preparing to implement the 1990 National Health Service and Community Care Act. It records the different ways in which they defined and approached the implementation task. It also analyses some central elements and implications of the policy to create a social care market.

The study was commissioned by the Department of Health Research and Development Division. This book has also been informed by work conducted by its authors on behalf of the Economic and Social Research Council, the Social Services Inspectorate, the National Health Service Training Directorate and the National Health Service Management Executive. We are grateful to all these bodies and most especially to our Department of Health Liaison Officers, Sue Moylan and Jenny Griffin.

Colleagues within the Nuffield Institute for Health and the Personal Social Services Research Unit have also been generous with their support and advice. We would like to thank Steve Carter, Jules Forder and Shane Kavanagh for their help with statistical analyses in Chapter 3, and Jules Forder and Jeremy Kendall for their comments on Chapter 6. Charlotte Armour and Maureen Weir yet again met our impossible demands for typing and re-typing the manuscript with their usual but remarkable tolerance and efficiency. Jane Dennett produced the final typeset text and, more importantly, coordinated and contributed to the editing of the final manuscript. Her tolerance and efficiency was, likewise, remarkable.

We are grateful to all the above for their assistance. Finally, however, we owe a real debt of gratitude to the local authority officers and members, and those people working in the National Health Service and the private and voluntary sectors, who gave their time and support so fully and willingly in the midst of such enormous changes. Research of this sort is simply impossible without such support.

1

Introduction: historical and policy context

The management and delivery of community care in the United Kingdom are currently undergoing their most substantial changes since the beginning of the post-war welfare state. If fully implemented, the government's policies will result in a fundamental transformation of the role of social services departments.

Such far-reaching changes will not take place overnight, and the government has recognized that the agenda outlined in its White Paper, *Caring for People*, is one set for at least a decade. The changes formally came into effect in April 1993, when central government transferred significant new responsibilities and resources to local government social services departments. Such an event was remarkable. It cut against the grain of policies which, for well over a decade, had sought to reduce the role of local authorities and to constrain their resource base. The occasion for this development was the final stage in the phased implementation of the NHS and Community Care Act 1990, under which the Department of Social Security ceased to be the source of public funding for the care of people entering private and voluntary residential or nursing homes. In its place, local authority social services departments took on responsibility for assessing the needs of, and purchasing appropriate care for, those who would previously have looked to the social security system to finance their care.

Although the local authority associations questioned the adequacy of the resources transferred to them for this purpose (House of Commons Health Committee 1993a), the funds involved are substantial. Over the three years 1993/94 to 1995/96, they build up to a total of £1,568 million a year, a figure equivalent to some 32 per cent of the 1992/93 budget estimates for current expenditure by all social services departments in England (House of Commons Health Committee 1993b). Perhaps not surprisingly, these sums were not transferred to social services departments without a number of constraints being placed upon how they could be spent. Most notably, departments were required to spend 85 per cent of the first year's transfer on services in the independent sector (Department of Health 1992a). That requirement does, of course, begin to explain this apparently uncharacteristic act of government policy towards local government: a central feature of the new responsibilities for social services departments is to reduce their role as direct service providers and, in its place, to develop their function as purchasers of social care.

This development was not an entirely new one in the sense that the statutory sector had never been the sole provider of social care. Indeed, the vast majority of such care has been – and continues to be – provided by relatives, friends and other sources of what is generally termed informal care. In addition, voluntary and private sector suppliers were established to such a degree that a mixed economy of social care already existed in some services – especially residential services to elderly people – and in many geographical areas. Similarly, as described in Chapter 2, there has long been a broad consensus that social services departments should adopt an 'enabling' role, actively stimulating and organizing a more diverse range of supply and suppliers. There were, of course, differences of view about the range and balance of suppliers and the nature of the enabling role, but the concepts themselves had well-established roots in the personal social services and could be shown to be consistent with good practice.

However, it would be misleading to overstate the degree of continuity in the roles and responsibilities of social services departments following the community care legislation. It would also be misleading to understate the 'cultural' revolution which this legislation implies for traditional ways of working (see, for example, Audit Commission 1992a, b). Moreover, one of the most fundamental aspects of this revolution is the development by social services departments of purchasing and contracting functions within what has increasingly come to be described as a social care market rather than merely a mixed economy. This emerging market orientation was much less consistent with established ideas about the role of social services departments and this aspect of the changes is discussed at greater length in subsequent chapters. For the present, it is sufficient to note that the principal theme of this book is how those departments began to understand and prepare for their roles as enablers under the terms of the community care legislation and related Department of Health guidance. As will become evident, relatively loose formulations and exhortations about promoting a mixed economy were superseded by clearer requirements to establish and manage a market in social care. This, in turn, implied a knowledge and skills base almost entirely lacking in the personal social services; it was also incompatible with many of the dominant political and professional values that had shaped their organization and management. Before we develop such themes further, however, it is necessary to sketch the principal elements of the community care changes and their evolution.

A chronology of community care

In one of the most comprehensive reviews of the long history and evolution of community care, Turrell (1991) traced the term back as far as the Wood report of 1929. Discussions of its varied meanings and emphases may be found elsewhere (see, for example, Department of Health and Social Security 1981; Walker 1982; Wistow 1983; Wistow and Henwood 1991; Knapp *et al.* 1992a). In addition, an analysis of the central dimensions of current community care policy may be found in Chapter 2. The focus of what follows here, therefore, is the emergence of the policy framework enshrined in the 1990 Act and subsequent guidance. Both the development and implementation of this framework have been long drawn out, complex and – apparently almost until the last moment (Brown 1992) – uncertain in their outcome. Some of the essential stepping stones in this policy-making process are identified in Box 1.1, although it would be possible to trace aspects of the policy's origins at least as far back as the Seebohm report (1968), as Utting (1990) has noted elsewhere. In this account, we do not aim to provide a blow-by-blow account of the policy's development but rather to identify a number of key themes and issues which shaped its formulation during the second half of the 1980s.

The first and most fundamental of these themes is the re-emergence in the mid-1980s of community care as a prominent feature of public policy. The Social Services Committee report (House of Commons Social Services Committee 1985a) was instrumental in placing community care on the policy agenda: the following year's report from the Audit Commission (1986) ensured that it has remained there ever since. The significance of these reports and

---

Box 1.1 *Caring for People*: a chronology of policy formulation

1985 House of Commons Social Services Select Committee report, *Community Care*

1985 Scott-Whyte report, *Supplementary Benefit and Residential Care*

1986 Audit Commission report, *Making a Reality of Community Care*

1987 Firth report, *Public Support for Residential Care*

1987 National Audit Office report, *Community Care Developments*

1988 Griffiths report, *Community Care: Agenda for Action*

1989 July statement by Kenneth Clarke on Griffiths

1989 White Paper, *Caring for People*

the importance of their origins in bodies independent of government is well-illustrated by the contrast between their focus and that of the 'Progress in Partnership' working party, which was established by the Department of Health, with the health and local authority associations, at the same time as the Select Committee's enquiry. In particular, the working party's remit effectively precluded it from examining underlying policy assumptions or the adequacy of resources: instead, its task was to examine the essentially second-order issue of how to improve joint planning. Hence, the core of its proposals was for 'an engine to drive joint planning' and its report contained forty-four detailed recommendations to achieve that end (Working Group on Joint Planning 1985: i; see also Westland 1988; Wistow 1988). By contrast, the Select Committee and, especially, the Audit Commission expressed more fundamental concerns about the nature and effectiveness of the underlying policy itself.

The Commission's general concern with effectiveness led it to question how far community care objectives were being achieved. Consequently, its report shifted the emphasis from policy means to policy ends; from the technicalities of joint planning to the nature of community care objectives and the extent to which they were being achieved. Moreover, with its statutory remit to investigate the impact of central government policies on local authorities, the Commission also shifted the emphasis from the failure of local agencies to collaborate effectively to the responsibility of central government for that failure (Wistow 1988: 74).

The shift in focus from a preoccupation with the mechanics of joint working between health and local authorities to the more effective delivery of community care objectives highlights a second broad theme to emerge from the documents listed in Box 1.1. In one way or another, each of them identifies community care as an area of *policy failure*. Perhaps the most critical is the Audit Commission's report (1986), which identified a pattern of 'slow and uneven progress' owing to a number of 'fundamental underlying problems', themselves reflecting 'policy contradictions' and 'perverse incentives' for which central government bore substantial responsibility. Briefly, these underlying problems comprised:

- disincentives for local authorities to invest in community care caused by a mismatch between policy objectives and funding systems;
- lack of bridging finance to support the shift from hospitals to care in the community;
- perverse incentives from an income support system which supported care in residential and nursing homes but not in other settings;
- organizational fragmentation and confusion in the responsibilities of agencies at all levels; and
- staffing problems resulting from the absence of workforce planning and effective staff training for community care.

The conclusions drawn by the Commission from its analysis were expressed in blunt terms, warning that 'if nothing changes the outlook is bleak' (*ibid.*: para. 48). Thus, it foresaw the possibility of 'a continued waste of resources and, worse still, care and support that is either lacking entirely or inappropriate to the needs of some of the most disadvantaged members of society and the relatives who seek to care for them' (*ibid.*: 5). It called on the government to institute radical change, therefore, and emphasized that 'the one option which is not tenable is to do nothing' (*ibid.*: 4). To help promote such change, it called for a high-level review and identified three strategic options worthy of consideration by such a review. These options included major reallocations of responsibility between health and local authorities in the case of mental health, learning disability and physical disability. Even more radically, it proposed joint board arrangements in the case of services to elderly people in the community.

In the wake of this penetrating and authoritative critique, the government did, indeed, commission a high-level review, though one with more limited terms of reference than those implied by the Commission. Thus, Sir Roy Griffiths, the Prime Minister's personal adviser on health service matters, was asked to lead an enquiry into community care. He was the author of an earlier – and highly critical – report on the organization and management of the NHS (Griffiths 1983). This report was immediately accepted by Ministers, and a general management system was swiftly introduced throughout the service. However, such rapid action was not to follow his report on community care, *Agenda for Action* (Griffiths 1988). Its tone was no less critical than his health service report and Griffiths identified the theme of policy failure in uncompromising terms. Accepting that all the 'essential facts' were contained in the reports of the Social Services Committee, the Audit Commission and the National Audit Office (1987), he argued that 'in few areas can the gap between political rhetoric and policy on the one hand, or between policy and reality in the field have been so great' (Griffiths 1988: iv).

Although precluded by his terms of reference from examining the adequacy of the resources allocated to community care, in another memorable phrase he appeared to be not entirely unsympathetic with the views of those critical about the adequacy of funding:

> The Audit Commission on the one hand were satisfied that better value could be obtained from existing resources. On the other hand, many social services departments and voluntary groups grappling with the problems at local level certainly felt that the Israelites faced with the requirement to make bricks without straw had a comparatively routine and possible task. (Griffiths 1988: iii)

He was also emphatic about the need for there to be a match between policy objectives and resources. Otherwise, he implied, community care was left in the worst of all possible worlds: 'if we try to pursue unrealistic policies the resources will be spread transparently thin' (*ibid.*: ix). Hence he 'insisted' that it was necessary to be 'open as to what we are trying to achieve and realistic as to what policies can be pursued with the likely available money. What cannot be acceptable is to allow ambitious policies to be embarked upon without the appropriate funds' (*ibid.*: ix).

As already noted, his terms of reference required him to focus on the utilization rather than the adequacy of resources. More specifically, he had been asked 'to review the way in which public funds are used to support community care policy and to advise [the Secretary of State] on the options for action which would improve the use of these funds as a contribution to more effective community care' (Department of Health and Social Security 1986). The need to compare arrangements for funding residential and nursing homes with those for domiciliary care was specifically identified in his brief. Thus, Griffiths's terms of reference required him to focus on the social security system's funding of residential and nursing home care, something which the Audit Commission had already criticized for its creation of perverse incentives. This issue represents the third of the themes to be highlighted here as part of the background to the community care changes. Moreover, from the viewpoint of the government, and certainly from the perspective of public expenditure control, it was this issue that provided the most important spur to the reforms enacted in 1990.

There were two compelling reasons for addressing this issue. First, social security support was readily available to meet the costs of residential and nursing home care in the independent sector, whereas no such similar support existed for domiciliary services. This situation was plainly inconsistent with community care objectives. Second, unlike health and local authority budgets, social security payments were not cash limited. In December 1979, supplementary benefit paid to support individuals in residential and nursing home care provided by the independent sector amounted to £10 million (12,000 claimants). By May 1991 the level of income support for such people was estimated to be £1,872 million (231,000 claimants), and the total amount was estimated to reach £2,480 million (270,000 claimants) by April 1993 (House of Commons Social Security Committee 1991: para. 4; Hansard 1993). Moreover, these substantial increases in expenditure took place despite successive attempts by central government to restrict their rate of growth (Parker 1987; Wistow 1987a).

Partly as a result of this failure, Griffiths's was the third government-sponsored enquiry in as many years to review the issue. A joint central and local government working party had already identified three options for the future funding of residential care (Scott-Whyte 1985) and a similar body was established to investigate their feasibility. Its report (Firth 1987) was made available to Griffiths and provided him with a detailed technical input to his wider review. Griffiths himself considered the division of responsibilities between local authorities and social security for the funding of residential and domiciliary care to be a 'particularly pernicious split' (Griffiths 1988: para. 4.21). He sought to eliminate the perverse incentive towards residential care which this produced by recommending that a unified community care budget be allocated to local social services authorities in the form of a specific grant, principally composed of resources transferred from the social security system. This principle was adopted by the government and formed the basis for the financial arrangements ultimately introduced in 1993. Initially, however, the concept of a specific grant was firmly resisted by Ministers (House of Commons Social Services Committee 1990: paras 31–32) and it was not until October 1992 that the Secretary of State announced that a limited form of ringfencing would be introduced. Under these arrangements, funds are transferred from the social security budget in three annual instalments and are ringfenced for the first year of each annual transfer. Thereafter they are included in the overall revenue support grant and thus, in principle, are available to local authorities to use as they wish.

Alongside the critique of the organization and funding of community care at the macro or systems level was a parallel critique at the micro or individual user level. Once again, responsibilities were said to be confused and overlapping, accountabilities unclear and, most fundamentally, service delivery poorly related to individual need. Hence, a further underlying theme in the development of community care policy was the need to individualize service responses, that is, to ensure that their provision was tailored to the more systematically assessed needs and preferences of individual users and their carers. This theme was emphasized in the Audit Commission's general emphasis on the importance of flexible service responses, based upon a wide range of options. More specifically, it called for 'the adjustment of services to meet the needs of people rather than the adjustment of people to meet the needs of services' (Audit Commission 1986: para. 10). In addition, it highlighted the importance of seeing care provision as part of a wider care process embracing referral, assessment, prescription, provision and review (*ibid.*: para. 170). Similar concerns were voiced by Griffiths and developed into recommendations for the publication of care management arrangements which would take full account of user and carer preferences (Griffiths 1988: paras 1.3, 6.2–6.7). His proposals for individual and managed care became one of the basic building blocks for the service delivery system outlined in *Caring for People* (Secretaries of State 1989b).

The final policy development emerging during the late 1980s was closely related to the social security issue and also bore directly on the central themes of this book: the development of the mixed economy and the enabling role of local authority social services departments. This chapter opened by noting the apparent paradox of a Conservative government transferring responsibilities and resources to local authorities. Its action was consistent with the recommendations of both the Firth (1987) and Griffiths (1988) reports. However, those recommendations were the principal reason why neither document found immediate favour with the government and helped to explain the fifteen-month delay in the government's response to Griffiths (see Wistow and Henwood 1988). Griffiths's report was effectively a vote of confidence in the capacity of local authorities to take the lead role in community care. He argued that this responsibility should remain where it currently lay and that local authorities were 'best placed to assess local needs, set local priorities and monitor performance' (Griffiths 1988: para. 5.27).

At the same time, however, he proposed a major recasting of their role so that they would function as 'the designers, organizers and purchasers of non-health care services, and not primarily as direct providers, making the maximum possible use of voluntary and private sector bodies to widen consumer choice, stimulate innovation and encourage efficiency' (*ibid.*: para. 1.3.4). These anticipated benefits of the enabling role were repeated in the White Paper (Secretaries of State 1989b) as the central justification for the development of a more mixed economy. Both Griffiths's and the White Paper's treatment of the enabling role are covered more fully in Chapter 2. *Caring for People* was published in November 1989, four months after a statement to Parliament by the Secretary of State, Kenneth Clarke, announcing the government's response to Griffiths. The White Paper drew on each of the themes identified above:

- the definition of clear objectives for community care (see Box 1.2) as the starting point for a broadly based programme of initiatives and a template against which to measure their implementation;
- the need to respond to shortcomings in existing services and organizational systems;
- the ending of the perverse incentives inherent in the social security arrangements;
- individualized care provided through care managers with devolved budgets; and
- a lead role for local authorities defined in terms of their becoming enablers and purchasers in a mixed economy.

More specifically the White Paper can be seen to contain two distinct elements (Wistow 1990a; Wistow and Henwood 1991). First, it specified the outcomes for users that government policies are intended to promote. Its underlying purpose was described as promoting choice and independence, with a consequential emphasis on home-based care, personal development and a greater consumer voice. Second, it outlined a new framework for organizing and delivering care so as to maximize these outcomes for users. The latter framework, however, should be seen in terms of what it omitted as well as what it contained. As noted above, the proposal that resources should be allocated to local authorities by means of a ringfenced specific grant was not accepted by the government until almost immediately before the final stage of implementation, and then in a more limited and temporary form than Griffiths had proposed. Other differences related to the role of the Minister of Health, whom Griffiths envisaged setting national objectives and priorities which would form the basis for a costed programme of activity each year. It also envisaged that the specific grant would be made to authorities only if local plans had been submitted which, on the one hand, were compatible with national policy objectives and priorities and, on the other hand, showed evidence of collaborative planning between local authority and other agencies, especially those in the NHS. Thus the differences between the Griffiths and White Paper recommendations concerned the related issues of the role of central government and the arrangements for funding community care (Wistow and Henwood 1991).

If we leave such matters to one side, however, the White Paper may be analysed in terms of its logical progression from the broad values and principles about independence and choice, through six key objectives (Box 1.2) largely derived from those values and principles, to a set of means for achieving them. These means essentially operated at three levels: the macro (or service system) level; the micro (or individual user) level; and the inter-agency level. Thus the new framework may be summarized in the following terms (Wistow 1990a, b):

- the organization of service systems based on the separation of purchaser and provider functions, the promotion of a mixed economy and the creation of new providers operating in an external market;
- the organization of service delivery through systematic arrangements for

---

Box 1.2 The key objectives of *Caring for People*

The White Paper's underlying purpose was described as one of 'promoting choice and independence'. This purpose was reflected in six key objectives:

- Promoting the development of domiciliary, day and respite services to enable people to live in their own homes wherever feasible and sensible
- Ensuring that service providers make practical support for carers a high priority
- Making proper assessment of need and good case management the cornerstone of high quality care
- Promoting the development of a flourishing independent sector alongside good quality public services
- Clarifying the responsibilities of agencies, so making it easier to hold them to account for their performance
- Securing better value for taxpayers' money by introducing a new funding structure for social care

Box 1.3   Phased implementation programme

Stage 1: April 1991

Financial
- new Specific Grant for Mental Illness
- new Specific Grant for Drugs and Alcohol

Implementation
- setting up inspection units
- setting up complaints procedures
- work to develop and implement the 'purchaser/provides' split

Developmental
- work on local authority and health authority plans
- continue with general development projects

Stage 2: April 1992

Implementation
- local authority and health authority plans

Developmental
- test out proposals on assessment/case management in preparation for the transfer of the care element of social security funding

Stage 3: April 1993

Financial
- transfer of social security for new cases after April 1993
- introduction of assessment and case management procedures

Source: Letter to Regional Health Authority Chairmen and Local Authority Social Services Committee Chairmen from the Minister for Health, Virginia Bottomley.

assessment, care management, devolved budgeting and, hence, some degree of decentralized purchasing;
- a re-emphasis on joint working through the clearer allocation of responsibilities for health and social care, combined with strengthened financial incentives for collaboration and a focus on planning outcomes rather than structures or processes.

The publication of the White Paper was swiftly followed by the appearance

---

Box 1.4   *Caring for People*: a chronology of policy implementation

1990   Decision to phase the Act's implementation

1990   Department of Health policy guidance on *Caring for People*

1991   Department of Health practice guidance (e.g. inspection, purchasing, assessment and care management)

1991   First RHA/SSI monitoring exercise (September)

1992   Foster/Laming letters (March and September)

1992   Establishment of community care support force (September)

1992   Secretary of State's Isle of Wight speech concerning financial arrangements and conditions (October)

---

of the NHS and Community Care Bill, and its enactment on 29 June 1990. The latter was, itself, almost immediately followed by a ministerial announcement (18 July) that full implementation would take place in three stages up to April 1993, rather than in its entirety in April 1991 as originally intended (see Box 1.3). The main reason for this delay was the need to hold down community charge levels (see Henwood *et al.* 1991) and its principal consequence was that the transfer of responsibilities and resources to local government was delayed until April 1993. The Secretary of State's announcement also argued that this delay would provide more time to prepare for implementation. Since then, the Department has funded a programme of development work and issued many volumes of guidance on implementation issues (see Box 1.4). Its approach was, first, to specify in the November 1990 policy guidance 'what' should be done in respect of each of the main elements of the new framework for organizing and delivering services: this included assessment and care management, community care planning, purchasing, inspection and complaints (Department of Health 1990a). Second, the Department produced more tightly specified advice on 'how' the changes should be implemented through the production of practice guidance from November 1991 onwards on the majority of the above issues. Third, it introduced a programme of monitoring implementation progress in every authority. This review process was conducted by regional health authorities and the regional officers of the Social Services Inspectorate. It was to be followed up later by the establishment in September 1992 of a 'Community Care Support Force' charged with the task of assisting authorities identified as giving 'significant cause for concern' about their implementation progress. Fourth, and as a direct consequence of these reviews, the Department sought to focus on those aspects of the legislation which had to be in place by April 1993. Thus two main requirements were identified in a letter issued jointly in March 1992 by Andrew Foster, the Deputy Chief Executive of the NHS, and Herbert Laming, the Chief Social

Services Inspector. These requirements were specified as: establishing arrange-ments for assessing care needs; and securing the provision of care, including residential and nursing home care (Department of Health 1992b: 2).

The letter further emphasized that 'obviously a key feature of [the above requirements] will be assessing and arranging appropriate care for new clients who would have been previously supported through the social security system' (*ibid*.: 2). To this end, it identified eight key tasks on which local authorities would need to concentrate, in collaboration with other agencies, in order to ensure that they reached a minimum state of preparedness by 1 April 1993. These tasks principally amounted to an elaboration of the two main require-ments, together with arrangements for involving family practitioner services, ensuring staff training and informing the public. (The NHS had separately been informed of four of them in previous guidance which described them as 'must be dones': Department of Health 1992d.)

The full significance of the Foster/Laming letter lay less in its detailed content than in the carefully incrementalist nature of the implementation strategy it signalled. That strategy may be characterized as one which focused on 'system maintenance' or, in the letter's own terminology, achieving 'a smooth transition to the new arrangements' (*ibid*.: 1). Consequently, many fundamental aspects of the changes were categorized as areas for 'continuing and longer-term development', including the development of care manage-ment and the further clarification of purchaser/provider roles within social services departments. Such an approach could be justified as realistic in relation to both the scale of the task implied by the overall reforms and the need to ensure continuity of provision during the change process. It was also consistent with the full title of the White Paper: *Caring for People – Community Care in the Next Decade and Beyond*. Up to this point, however, the implementation task had been conceived less in terms of preparations for implementing a programme of managed change over the medium to long term than in terms of securing what amounted to a comprehensive recasting of the organization and delivery of services overall. Prior to March 1992, little attention had been given to the relative priority and sequencing of different aspects of the reforms, other than as a result of the decision to implement them in three phases between 1991 and 1993. By contrast, however, that earlier decision had been essentially shaped by political and related financial imperatives rather than an assessment of the need for managed change. We explore further, in Chapter 2, some of the thinking which lay behind the emphasis on smooth transition in the first Foster/Laming letter, an approach which was reiterated six months later in a second letter from the same sources (Department of Health 1992c).

Plan of the book

Much of the remainder of this book is concerned with the initial steps taken by a sample of local authorities in their preparations for implementing the community care legislation and subsequent guidance. Its central focus is on how they interpreted and pursued the enabling role in terms of promoting and managing a mixed economy of care. The book is based on a study commissioned by the Department of Health. It had the initial aims of mapping the extent of the existing mixed economy and identifying local authority alternatives to and plans for developing greater diversity of supply. The study, which was conducted between 1990 and 1992, drew on two principal sources of data: documentary and interview materials in twenty-four local authorities supported by national statistical returns and other statistics about supply in statutory and non-statutory sectors. Further details of the research strategy are provided in the Appendix.

In the next chapter, we look in more detail at the origins of the enabling role for social services departments which lay at the core of both the White Paper and our research. Chapter 3 describes the mixed economy of social care in England prior to the implementation of the 1990 Act, using routinely available national statistics to illustrate that the mixed economy was already fairly well developed in one or two respects, but would be likely to alter markedly in the coming years. In Chapter 4 we examine authorities' initial responses to the legislative programme and associated guidance in terms of prevailing political and philosophical views and their detailed organizational arrangements. The practical steps that local authorities were taking to develop a mixed economy of care are examined in Chapter 5. The book then turns to opportunities for, and barriers to, the development of social care markets (Chapter 6). The expectations of local authorities and others as to the likely consequences of encouraging greater competition between providers in a market funded substantially by public sector contracts are analysed with reference to the criteria of costs, quality, choice and equity. In Chapter 7 we describe the findings of a detailed study (in a subsample of six authorities) of the perceived barriers and opportunities – especially the financial incentives – associated with the transfer of residential care homes to the 'independent' sector. Finally (in Chapter 8), we seek to explain the paradox at the heart of our findings between the universal support of an enabling role for social services departments, on the one hand, and the limited progress in implementing the White Paper's requirements, on the other.

2

Community care: markets and enabling

In the interval between the publication of the Griffiths report in March 1988 and *Caring for People* in November 1989, there was little argument about the desirability of creating a more mixed economy of care. Indeed, in advocating the acceptance of Griffiths's recommendations, the Association of Directors of Social Services emphasized that their departments were no longer monolithic service providers and that they welcomed the opportunity to take on more fully the role of enablers, promoting an increasingly mixed economy of care (Association of Directors of Social Services 1988). Challenges to this view were rare (for example, Jack 1990) and had little, if any, impact on the national policy debate. Significantly, the Labour Party's policy on community care at the 1992 general election concentrated on the need for 'a level playing field' to ensure fair competition between sectors, rather than a reassertion of public sector dominance in the provision of services (Labour Party 1992).

This apparently broad-based acceptance that social and community care should be delivered through a mixed economy of providers in the public and independent sectors did not mean that there was universal agreement about the nature and balance of suppliers within and between those sectors. However, the principle of greater diversity of supply appeared to be broadly accepted as a legitimate objective of policy. Integral to such support for provider pluralism was the notion that social services departments should adopt an enabling role. Again (and as this book demonstrates), a range of views existed about how this concept should be interpreted and its implications for both the management and service delivery tasks of social services departments. None the less, the enabling role had long-established roots in thinking about policy and practice in the personal social services. However, it should be added that the concept of enabling also had roots elsewhere in thinking about the role of central and local government more generally. It is important to recognize, therefore, that the organizational changes contained in *Caring for People* were not conceived in a vacuum; nor are they being implemented in isolation from wider policies towards the public sector. If we are to understand the nature of the mixed economy changes, together with the management tasks they imply, it is necessary to locate them within the context of those broader policies as well as the more specific context of the personal social services.

Enabling and public sector management

As the Audit Commission (1987: para. 1) has pointed out, the decision to make or to buy goods and services is among the most important that industrial and commercial organizations have to take. It is also a decision which government policy has sought to place at the heart of public sector management. Public agencies have, of course, always bought a diverse range of supplies and services. Initially, the influence of 'new right' neo-classical economics led the post-1979 Conservative administrations to extend that process through the contracting out of ancillary services such as catering and cleaning (Ascher 1987; Metcalfe and Richards 1990). Subsequently they extended it to those core services whose direct provision had been the defining purpose of most public sector organizations. Historically, public services were equated with both public funding and public provision; an equation which recent Conservative governments have done much to challenge. Their definition of a new purpose for public authorities was neatly expressed by a former Environment Secretary, who said that local authorities should adopt a role of 'enabling not providing' (Ridley 1988). Indeed, the notion that local authorities should be enablers rather than providers was fundamental to the review of local government initiated in 1991. For example, while acknowledging that local authorities would continue to have 'important...providing roles', the consultative document on their internal management emphasized that 'councils should be looking to contract out work to whoever can deliver services most efficiently and effectively' (Department of the Environment 1991: para. 4).

Thus, in the field of local government policy, the concept of enabling was equated with that of the 'competitive council' (Audit Commission 1988) and, consequently, with the introduction of market mechanisms into the supply of services in which a public sector monopoly had been a largely unchallenged policy assumption in the post-war period. As the Audit Commission (*ibid.*: para. 12) argued,

> it was...generally assumed that direct public provision was the best way of meeting the needs for most basic services. Council houses, schools, old people's homes and many other services replaced and rationalised the inadequate and uncoordinated efforts of the private and voluntary sectors,

and formed a virtual monopoly for large sections of the population...The word competition was almost never heard.

This situation was immediately challenged in the new Conservative administration's first programme of legislation. The principle of compulsory competitive tendering for building work was introduced by the Planning and Local Act of 1980 and extended to virtually all local authority direct labour work under the 1988 Local Government Act. The same year's Housing Act and Education Reform Act also shared the objective of diminishing the local authority role in direct service management and provision, albeit through the vehicle of service users choosing to 'opt out' of local authority control. Those council tenants who had not exercised the right to buy, granted under previous legislation, could collectively choose new landlords through the creation of not-for-profit housing action trusts. Similarly, parents could vote for their children's schools to 'opt out' of local education authority control and become directly funded ('grant maintained') by the Department for Education. The local management of schools, introduced under the same legislation, effectively devolved control over the largest element of local authority spending from Education Committees to headteachers and school governors. In addition, parental freedom of choice between schools combined with capitation funding to introduce quasi-market forces which were intended to reward popular schools and penalize less popular ones.

Comparable developments were evident outside local government. Changes adopted in the health service were not dissimilar, in their essentials, to those introduced in the schools system. Organizational responsibilities for funding and managing service delivery were separated through the purchaser/ provider split. Individual hospitals were encouraged to seek trust status outside the control of district health authorities and directly responsible to the Department of Health. Again, the new arrangements were intended to promote competition between providers and, thus, to provide new incentives for improved performance. In central government itself, the 'Next Steps' initiative (Efficiency Unit 1988) had similarly sought to separate responsibility for planning and management from traditional departmental structures through the creation of executive agencies. In the field of social policy, the creation of the Benefits Agency with responsibility for the management of the social security programme provides the most substantial example of a Next Steps agency. In the NHS, a similar concern to distinguish between responsibility for policy and management led to the establishment of a Policy Board and a Management Executive, respectively (Harrison et al. 1990). That the latter is not, however, a fully fledged Next Steps agency perhaps signifies a perceived need for ministers not to distance themselves too far from what is the most politically sensitive of all public services. More recently, in a further extension of the contracting-out principle, legislation has been introduced to provide for the market testing of most civil service responsibilities (the Civil Service (Management Functions) Bill 1992).

All these initiatives in central and local government show the influence of neo-liberal critiques of public bureaucracies as self-interested, budget-maximizing agencies, protected from competitive forces and, thereby, the necessary spurs to economy and efficiency which the market provides. Moreover, the various organizational responses identified above all imply a new range of skills and tasks for public sector managers, among which the ability to set up and manage contractual arrangements is the most central. As Jenkins (1992: 215) has noted,

> at the heart of the executive agency process is the development of 'frameworks' or contracts to define the operating relationship between a department and its agencies. These contracts have to set out the results the sponsoring department wants to achieve for its policies, the resources necessary to achieve those results and the method of evaluation.

Whether services are delivered through the independent or public sectors, therefore, their design and funding is increasingly specified and delivered through contracts or service agreements. These developments, in turn, require skills in setting standards, specifying services, awarding contracts, monitoring performance and taking action if performance falls short of specifications (Department of the Environment 1991: para. 5). Such a relationship underpins purchaser/provider roles in the NHS and, as we shall see, is an integral element in the framework through which social services departments are to manage the mixed economy of social care.

The neo-classical economists of the 'new right' have not been the only sources of thinking about enabling roles in the public sector, however. In particular, a concept of the enabling authority has been the centrepiece of a defence of public sector values in the sphere of local government (Clarke and Stewart 1988; Brooke 1989). It describes the new right concept of the enabling role as a 'minimalist view of local government' in which it retains only 'residual responsibilities' and its most important job is 'to pass on the doing' (Clarke and Stewart 1990: 5). By contrast, these authors elaborate an alternative conception of the enabling role closely related 'to the continental model of the local authority as the community governing itself', with a power of general competence which allows the authority 'to take action to meet needs and problems in the community regardless of whether there is a specific responsibility' (ibid.: 4).

Describing their approach as 'a reassertion of the role of local authorities as local government', Clarke and Stewart define this role as

> enabling the community to define and then to meet the needs and problems it faces. It neither requires the direct provision of services nor prescribes it...It will purchase some services itself. It will work with and through other organizations in the public, private and voluntary sectors – aiding, stimulating and guiding their contributions. (ibid.: para. 1.11)

This concept of enabling as local government does not, however, rule out contractual relationships with providers in the independent sector. To the extent that market mechanisms are supported, they are only one of many forms of relationship between local authorities and external agencies (Brooke 1989: 11).

Local government has, therefore, been a sphere in which two fundamentally different concepts of enabling have been developed. As a result, a collectivist, community-oriented approach has effectively competed alongside one based on market mechanisms. As we show in this book, the existence of these different understandings had significant implications for the way in which local authorities interpreted and responded to their new responsibilities for the mixed economy.

Enabling and the personal social services

Social care has been provided within a mixed economy throughout the lifetime of the personal social services. Although private, for-profit organizations have played a minimal role within that framework until comparatively recently, voluntary organizations have provided many services – albeit often in specialized areas – alongside campaigning and advisory roles. In addition, significant numbers of individuals have contributed to service provision in diverse ways as unpaid volunteers; and, most important, the bulk of caring responsibilities have been met by families, neighbours and friends. None the less, the mixed economy has become a more prominent feature of social and community care during the past decade and more especially since the mid-1980s. First, voluntary and private sector providers have increased their market share (Knapp 1989), particularly in the residential care sector where they have become the majority suppliers, almost exclusively as a result of substantial growth in the private sector and the liberalization of demand-side social security subsidies. (Further details of the various sectors' 'market shares' are to be found in Chapter 3.) Second, local voluntary organizations have become better organized and more self-confident contributors to local policy networks and service systems. The Wolfenden report (1978), *Working Together* (ACC, NCVO and AMA 1981) and the statutory requirement to include voluntary sector representatives in the joint planning arrangements (Department of Health and Social Security 1984) have all legitimated increased partnerships in policy-making, service development and service delivery processes, even if the results nationally have been uneven, and statutory authorities have remained the dominant partners. Third, the role of social services departments has been progressively redefined to emphasize their responsibility for both creating a mixed economy and managing it more systematically. Aspects of the latter functions were identified in governmental and quasi-governmental sources during the 1980s, including the Barclay report (1982), Norman Fowler's (1984) Buxton speech, the Griffiths report (1988), and the *Caring for People* White Paper (Secretaries of State 1989b). They were also prefigured in the Seebohm report's (1968) emphasis on social planning and the community dimension of the role of social services departments (see also Utting 1990; Wistow 1992a).

While the 'enabling' theme repeatedly appeared in these sources, its meaning has evolved and developed over time. Seebohm, Barclay and, to a considerable extent, Fowler were essentially concerned with social services departments mobilizing and sustaining the fullest possible contributions to care from the resources of local communities, including informal carers. It was, however, Fowler's Buxton speech that brought the terminology of enabling to the centre of discussion about the future of the personal social services. In that speech he advanced the concept of enabling as 'fundamental to the role of social services departments that the government wished to promote'. Accordingly, and in a reassessment of Seebohm, Fowler advocated 'a wider conception of social services' in which the fundamental role of the state was to back up and develop the assistance which is given to private and voluntary support. Consequently, the state should seek to tap the 'great reservoir of voluntary and private effort' and, thereby, enable people to 'give something back to their own local community by participating in social support'. It was an approach consonant with the Thatcherite themes of self-help, individual responsibility and what Fowler's successor (John Moore) was to describe in 1987 as 'the long evolutionary march of the welfare state...from dependence to independence' (quoted in McCarthy 1989: 25).

Against this background, Fowler identified 'three paramount responsibilities' for social services departments: first, to take a comprehensive strategic view of all the sources of care available in their area; second, to recognize that the direct provision of services was only part of the local pattern and that other forms of provision were available and to be worked out; and, third, to see a major part of its function as promoting and supporting the fullest possible participation of the other different sources of care that existed or could be called into being. Thus, the Fowler version of the enabling role emphasized the strategic tasks of mobilizing new sources of care and coordinating their delivery. It particularly focused on encouraging private individuals and local communities to contribute to the provision of care. Such echoes of Seebohm and Barclay meant that Fowler was advancing concepts that were – or could be seen to be – both familiar and broadly acceptable to the statutory personal social services. They were also largely consistent with thinking about the wider role of local government as community governance advocated by Stewart (1974 1986). Ironically, however, at the same time that these ideas were beginning to become established in local government circles through the 'enabling authority' concept, described above, the Griffiths report (1988) set in motion a new and radically different set of influences on the management of social services departments.

The publication of Griffiths's report marked the beginning of a shift towards a definition of enabling far less compatible with the established values of social work and social care but much more consistent with the promotion of market mechanisms elsewhere in the public sector. Thus, Griffiths went considerably beyond the Buxton speech by introducing the concept of social services departments as the purchasers of social care within a market place of competing providers. Their functions were summarized as

> designers, organisers and purchasers of non-health care services and not primarily as direct providers, making the maximum possible use of voluntary and private sector bodies to widen consumer choice, stimulate innovation and encourage efficiency. (*ibid.*: para. 1.3.4)

This purchasing function was not further defined by Griffiths. However, his recommendations were of fundamental significance in requiring social services authorities to maximize choice and competition through the development of private services (*ibid.*: para. 6.9) as well as to continue to develop and sustain voluntary and informed care. In these respects, therefore, Griffiths can be seen to be looking back to the traditional emphasis in the personal social services on enabling as the stimulation of community resources while also looking forward to the new world of purchasers and providers.

As noted above, Fowler's version of the mixed economy stressed the role of community and voluntary resources. To the extent that private care was mentioned, the stress was on private individuals rather than the organized, for-profit organizations. Griffiths (1988: para. 3.2) did, of course, underwrite the role of informal care as 'the primary means by which people are enabled to live normal lives in community settings'; but he went beyond the conventional encouragement of private individuals to assume more responsibility for providing informal care by promoting private businesses as alternative providers of formal care. He argued that 'the onus in all cases should be on the social services authorities to show that the private sector is being fully stimulated and encouraged and that competitive tenders and other means of testing the market are being taken' (*ibid.*: vii). Central government funding would be conditional, in part, on departments demonstrating that such functions were being fulfilled and that voluntary and private sector providers were increasing their market shares.

Between the publication of the Griffiths report (March 1988) and *Caring for People* (November 1989) the Department of Health made a more explicit distinction between purchasing and providing functions in its radical proposals for change in the NHS, referred to above. The White Paper *Working for Patients* (Secretaries of State 1989a) aimed to create a largely internal market in which health authorities purchased services from provider units, NHS trusts and, to a lesser extent, the independent sector (Harrison 1991; Wistow 1992b). The purchaser/provider distinction was the fundamental organizational principle on which the NHS changes were founded. It was, therefore, no surprise that the same principle was transferred by the same department and ministers to the organization and management of community care. The result was a new concept of enabling: *Caring for People* described the responsibilities of social services departments as 'securing the delivery of services, not simply by acting as direct providers but by developing the purchasing and contracting role to become "enabling authorities" ' (Secretaries of State 1989b: para. 3.1.3). Moreover, the White Paper's six key objectives included that of promoting the development of a flourishing independent sector alongside good-quality public services (para. 1.11). To this end, social services authorities were 'to make maximum possible use of private and voluntary providers' (*ibid.*). The role of the new enabling social services departments was further outlined in terms of:

- 'determining clear specifications of service requirements, and arrangements for tenders and contracts;
- taking steps to stimulate the setting up of 'not-for-profit' agencies;
- identifying areas of their own work which are sufficiently self-contained to be suitable for 'floating off' as self-managing units; and
- stimulating the development of new voluntary sector activity' (*ibid.*: para. 3.4.6).

In addition, they were also required to give priority to 'developing purchasing systems for private residential and nursing home care' (para. 3.4.8). Thus, the enabling role envisaged by the White Paper included three central elements: separation of purchasing and providing functions to at least some degree within social services departments; development and support of increased levels of activity by private and not-for-profit providers; and the regulation of provider agencies in all sectors – including the public sector – through a process of service specification and contracting. These latter activities, conducted within the framework provided by needs-led community care plans and planning agreements, formed the core processes through which social services departments were to manage the mixed economy in the post-White Paper world.

The purpose of stimulating the development of non-statutory service providers was expressed in terms of benefits to consumers and in particular: a wider range of choice; more flexible and innovatory ways of meeting individual needs; and better value for money resulting from competition between providers (para. 3.4.3). The White Paper also expressed the view that the evolutionary development of service specifications, tendering, agency agreements and contracts would produce further benefits by requiring authorities to: define desired outcomes; be more specific about the design of services to achieve those outcomes; and define the necessary inputs (para. 3.4.7). Such developments were seen, in turn, to require an improvement in information systems and what the White Paper called a 'more vigorous approach to management' based on the clear distinction between purchasing and providing functions (para. 3.4.8). These requirements recall – and are reinforced by – Griffiths's scathing criticisms of

> the present lack of refined information systems and management accounting within any of the authorities to whom one might look centrally or locally to be responsible for community care [which] would plunge most

organizations in the private sector into a quick and merciful liquidation. This has in any case to be remedied in the interests of an effective service. (Griffiths 1988: para. 29, viii)

The development of such a purchasing function implied major changes in the organization of departments which historically had had an administrative rather than a management culture (Social Services Inspectorate 1990). Indeed, they required a strengthening of precisely those activities which had hitherto been most seriously underdeveloped in the planning and management of social services departments: the identification of needs, service design, service application and performance review (Wistow 1990a). Moreover, in advocating enabling as a purchasing role, the White Paper was requiring departments to take on responsibilities for which they were ill-equipped while simultaneously divesting themselves, at least in part, of the provider role which had traditionally been their area of relative managerial strength.

Behind the apparent continuity suggested by the enabling terminology, therefore, lay a major break with previous policies for the personal social services. Although compulsory competitive tendering was explicitly rejected in the White Paper, its underlying objective was similar. The concept of the enabling authority which evolved through Seebohm, Barclay and Fowler had effectively been overlain by that of the 'competitive council' (Audit Commission 1987) which had emerged from a different debate about public sector management in general and local government management in particular. The emphasis shifted from mobilizing informal and community resources to developing a social care market in which the private sector was a significant provider of formal services. Its inevitable consequence was that market development and market management would become key responsibilities for social services departments. Not only were these responsibilities for which, as indicated above, departments had little or no relevant experience but, as many subsequently argued, they were incompatible with the nature and value base of social care. In studying the development and management of the mixed economy we are, therefore, not only exploring how social services departments defined and understood new roles, but also how they began to prepare for a process of substantial change in their organizational culture.

Community care and strategic change

Community care is the broad policy context within which the enabling role of social services departments is being developed. In Chapter 1 we outlined the background to, and reasons for, the major policy changes incorporated in *Caring for People*. We also noted there the contribution of the White Paper in clarifying policy objectives in a field marked by both ambiguity and implementation failure. The lack of clarity about community care – the differing and sometimes widely divergent understandings, objectives and priorities embraced within the one term – have been too frequently rehearsed to require detailed consideration here (see, for example, Titmuss 1968; Department of Health and Social Security 1981; Walker 1982; Webb and Wistow 1982; Wistow 1983; Bulmer 1987; Knapp *et al.* 1992a). One of the explanations for the existence of wide variations in understanding and interpretation is that they reflect real differences in ideological positions, beliefs and values: for example, feminist, professional, resource management, collectivist and individualist perspectives on community care lead to different definitions and emphases. Second, however, a degree of ambiguity may be considered functional in some quarters: clarity of purpose and direction would lead, as Griffiths intended, to clarity of responsibilities and accountabilities. It is, therefore, perhaps no accident that many of the elements of the Griffiths report which central government chose not to accept would have had the effect of defining its own roles and responsibilities more explicitly (Wistow and Hardy 1993).

A further explanation for the lack of clarity about the purposes and objectives of community care is that the policy is, in effect, a moving target, constantly being shaped and reshaped in the light of experience or fashion. For example, Wistow and Henwood (1991) have suggested that traditional definitions of community care are notable for emphasizing the location or source of assistance (care in and care by the community, respectively). By contrast, such definitions are being overtaken by approaches derived from Wolfensberger's (1977) normalization principles. Such principles give more prominence to organizing services around individual needs and being more explicit about personal outcomes or accomplishments (O'Brien 1986) that services are intended to secure. In particular, they emphasize the rights to participate in socially valued lifestyles which maximize opportunities for self-realization and independence. Thus they support, and reinforce, a concept of enabling as personal growth and development which has long underpinned social work. The underlying aims of *Caring for People* strongly reflect the influences of enabling conceived in such terms, the changes outlined within it being intended to:

- enable people to live as normal a life as possible;
- help them achieve the maximum possible independence and their full potential; and
- give them a greater individual say in how they live their lives and the services they need to help them to do so. (Secretaries of State 1989b: para. 1.8)

In setting out these principles and its six key objectives for service delivery (see Chapter 1), the White Paper represented a significant clarification of the meaning and purpose of community care policy. In so doing, it provided a framework for the design of service delivery systems and a template against which their outputs and outcomes could be evaluated. The process of securing those aims and objectives through the organizational changes proposed in the White Paper is, however, extremely complex in at least three respects: the

---

Box 2.1   Strategic dimensions of change

Institutional services   . . . . Community services

Supply-led services   . . . . Needs-led services

Public sector provision   . . . . Independent sector provision

NHS auspices   . . . . Local government auspices

---

extent of change; variations in the capacity and willingness of local authorities to implement change; and uncertainties surrounding the development and management of the social care market. Such complexities are better understood if we disaggregate the implementation task into its component parts. Box 2.1 identifies four strategic dimensions of change. Reduced to their basics, they may be described in the following terms:

- The first concerns the need to find the most appropriate balance between institutional and community services, with the thrust of policy being to shift the balance away from the former (including hospital, residential and nursing homes) to appropriately-planned and well-funded arrangements for the latter.
- Second is the move away from supply-led, provider-dominated services to needs-led, purchaser-dominated services over which individual users have significantly greater influence, and within which carers have well-defined, participative roles.
- The third concerns the balance between public and independent sector provision within an increasingly mixed economy of supply, on the one hand, and a more unified budget for social care, on the other. The latter has implications for the continued expansion of user choice while the former highlights the importance of independent regulatory functions.
- The fourth key dimension focuses on the balance of funding and providing responsibilities between the NHS and local government, respectively, with some client group and purchasing responsibilities moving to the latter.

In practice (if only implicitly), national policy development and implementation requirements in this field have been concerned with achieving appropriate balances along and between each dimension to promote user welfare and systems efficiency. Thus, for its part, *Caring for People* may be seen as designed to secure developments along each of those dimensions in a left-to-right direction on Box 2.1. Concerted movement along those dimensions not only implies a substantial management of change agenda but also the need for managed change to ensure both a smooth transition into the new arrangements and continuity of provision for existing users.

Two further layers of complexity may also be identified here. First, there is considerable variation at local level both in the starting points for change along each of those dimensions and in views about where the end point should lie. This consideration reflects the fact that community care is a local as well as a national policy. For example, local authorities have different views – reflecting local political values and priorities – about the appropriate balance between the statutory and independent sectors and the desirable mix between for-profit and not-for-profit providers. In addition, health and local authorities have differing views about the desirable balance between their own responsibilities, views which are influenced by service and resource stocks and also by professional interests.

A final element of complexity derives from the nature of change that movement along the policy dimensions implies. It has become conventional wisdom that *Caring for People* requires a major transformation of service systems and organizational cultures (see, for example, Audit Commission 1992b). To take only one example, the objective of developing needs-led services based upon individual needs assessment and care packaging is generally described in terms of developing a wider range of more flexible and responsive services. Current service systems, it is accepted, depend upon too narrow a range of standardized units of provision into which users are slotted rather like round pegs in square holes. Less frequently discussed are the implications of such thinking for the management of change and especially how resources can be moved from present to new service structures without destabilizing current provider systems and damaging continuity of care for individual users. Such considerations are particularly important in relation to the new assessment and purchasing responsibilities which local authorities assumed in April 1993. An examination of the nature of the market created by these changes enables us to explore more fully the crucial importance of securing a process of managed change which enables a smooth transition along each of the policy dimensions identified here.

Developing the social care market

Our earlier analysis suggested that, behind the apparent continuity implied by the terminology of enabling, *Caring for People* represented a real break with the past for the personal social services in terms of the relationship between funding and provision. Most particularly, its longer-term objective to promote a more vigorous independent sector points towards the substantial injection of market mechanisms into social care. We suggested above that this version of enabling had emerged from a debate about the future role of local government more broadly, rather than that of social services departments, and reflected a still broader set of policies towards the role and management of the public

sector as a whole. In addition, the Department of Health's policies towards
the NHS had been influential in the detail of the new arrangements. The end
result was a shift in emphasis from a focus on the mobilization of informal
and community resources to the development of a social care market in which
both private and voluntary sectors would be major providers. In turn, this
emphasis implied that market development and market management were to
be central responsibilities of social services departments. While social services
departments had long contracted with the independent sector in the fields of,
for example, specialist residential services for children and adults, such services
remained a small element of the overall provision, as we show in Chapter 3.
More fundamentally, social services departments had never before had the
responsibility for creating and managing a market.

As indicated above, the form and language of *Caring for People*'s proposals
reflected their origins in the Department of Health rather than the Department
of the Environment. However, the social care market differed fundamentally
from that which had been proposed for the NHS earlier the same year
(Secretaries of State 1989a). Health authorities became responsible for purchasing services to meet the needs of their resident populations through
contracts with provider units. The provider function, itself, was initially devolved to arm's-length direct service organizations (directly managed units)
and a small number of NHS trusts, with independent corporate status. By
April 1994, most of the provider units will have successfully applied for the
latter status (Department of Health 1993a). However, the supply of health
services remains a predominantly public sector responsibility and competition
is largely restricted to that taking place within an internal market. While
sharing some common features with this model, the social care market was
fundamentally different in implying the creation of an 'external' rather than
an internal market. Large parts of the supply system in social care were already
within the independent sector and social services departments were required
to stimulate it further. As a result, social services departments faced greater
complexity than health authorities in terms of both creating and managing a
market. Whether the nature and complexities of this role were fully appreciated
in 1989 at either local or national level is doubtful.

The social care market does, however, share with that in the health
service some aspects of what Williamson (1975) termed 'quasi markets' (see
also Le Grand 1990). Compared with textbook markets, services continue to
be publicly funded and purchases are made not directly by consumers but on
their behalf by, for example, general practitioners and care managers. Some
degree of direct purchasing is possible, however, in the social care market.
Individual consumers (or more probably their relatives and friends) are per-
mitted to 'top up' payments by social services departments if they choose to
live in more expensive residential and nursing home care (Department of
Health 1992e). This is specifically forbidden in the NHS, although the private
purchase of both health and social care has been growing during the past
decade.

The health and social care markets also differ from conventional ones in that competition takes place between providers in the public as well as the independent sectors. The objective of the NHS changes is to establish a market in which services not only continue to be publicly funded but are also almost entirely publicly provided. This approach reflects both political and pragmatic considerations: the high costs of capital-intensive, high-technology medicine limit market entry by independent sector providers while political concern about the privatization of health care has effectively precluded changes in the ownership of existing provider units. In short, it is the nature of funding and accountability relationships which was changed through the introduction of market mechanisms in the NHS rather than the ownership of the provider function.

By contrast, the social care changes seek to promote a shift in the ownership of supply as well as a change in the relationship between funding and supply. Compared with the internal market in health care based on existing suppliers, the external market in social care will depend on expanding supply in the independent sector. It might be argued that there is already oversupply in the case of residential (and nursing home) care, where the total volume of private and voluntary provision now exceeds that in the statutory sector (see Chapter 3). However, the growth of the independent sector has been geographically uneven between and within localities. In addition, the funding arrangements flowing from *Caring for People* are explicitly designed to make the purchase of residential services financially more attractive than direct service provision (House of Commons Health Committee 1993a). Both these factors mean that some social services departments may have to continue to stimulate non-statutory sector residential and nursing provision, if only in the medium term.

The principal task, however, will be to stimulate independent sector provision in other areas of service – domiciliary, day and respite care – where direct services remain the major source of supply. In such cases, meeting the White Paper's objective of developing a thriving independent sector necessarily implies a major shift in the ownership of supply, whether by 'hiving off' existing provision or by encouraging new suppliers to enter the market. Second, this imperative is reinforced by the White Paper's fundamental objective of shifting the balance between such services and the residential sector. In other words, social services departments are being required to secure an expansion of provision in precisely those areas in which the independent sector is currently most weak and in which, therefore, there are fewest foundations on which to build. Managing the tension between the mixed economy and 'community services' dimensions of the White Paper's strategy for community care does, therefore, constitute a double layer of complexity for social services departments.

At the same time, and alongside this combined service and market development task, the social security changes place on social service departments new responsibilities for market management in the residential care sector. Until now, departments have had little or no role in creating or managing the mixed economy of residential care which emerged as the un-planned and accidental consequence of changes in the social security system. In the absence of similar sources of funding for alternatives to residential care, the social security system had effectively underwritten a pattern of service growth and development which was the reverse of that intended by govern-ment policy (Wistow 1987a). In addition, social security expenditure in support of institutional care was imprecisely targeted on need (Bradshaw 1988) and proved difficult to control. In the first place, entitlement to benefit was established by an assessment of financial means rather than of the need for care. Second, such benefits were demand-led rather than cash-limited and continued to grow rapidly, notwithstanding repeated attempts to limit their increase (see Chapter 1).

From 1993, the 'care element' of those payments is being transferred to local authorities over a four-year period as a cash-limited special transitional grant. At the end of each year, however, the grant is subsumed within the general revenue support grant (see House of Commons Health Committee 1993a). In turn, social services departments have responsibility for purchasing residential and nursing home provision from that date for those individuals assessed as being in need of such care. Where their needs may be met more appropriately by domiciliary and other services, the transferred resources are available for such purposes. These changes are intended to enable more flexi-bility in the allocation of public funds between different kinds of services in response to systematic assessments of individual needs, while also bringing such spending within cash limit disciplines. In effect, demand-side subsidies to individuals based on their financial needs are to be replaced by supply-side (purchasing) decisions based on need and made by care managers with defined budgets. Moreover, social services departments will be required to manage a market which they have played little, if any, part in creating and in the the light of overarching policy objectives which are expected to lead to a con-traction in the overall scale of institutional provision. Some degree of 'misplace-ment' in institutional care is expected to be eliminated by the introduction of individual needs-based assessments while the expansion of alternative services is also expected to reduce demand for institutional care through the provision of real choice between alternatives.

In the light of the above analysis, we may summarize in the following terms the characteristics of the social care market which social services depart-ments are being required to develop and manage.

- First, it is to be a largely public-funded, but external, market in which public sector provision will decrease compared with that of the independent sector.
- Second, service development objectives require an expansion of alternatives to institutional care and, thus, of the kinds of services which remain largely underdeveloped in the private and voluntary sectors.

- Third, that part of the market in which independent sector supply is already strongly established will also be the one in which some contraction of supply is expected.
- Fourth, although financial incentives have been put in place to encourage a reduction in public sector residential services, the social security changes nevertheless represent a major shift in market conditions. As such, they can be expected to affect the confidence of independent providers about the continuity of funding in what will for the first time be a publicly managed market.

The transition to the new funding and assessment arrangements and also to a new balance of institutional and home-based care will not be a painless one. It is likely to threaten the stability of both supply and, in consequence, continuity of care for individual residents. Given that social services departments have almost no experience of market management, an inherently difficult task assumes even greater proportions. Nor is the relative smoothness of transition only of consequence for the personal social services and their users. The interdependence of health and social care systems ensures that the NHS has substantial interests in the operation of the new social care market. The Department of Health has estimated that among the 100,000 people who might have been expected to enter publicly funded long-stay residential and nursing home care in England during 1993/94 if social security responsibilities had remained unchanged, some 40,000 would have been discharged from hospitals (Laming 1992). Any disruption to those discharge patterns would have inescapable consequences for the NHS in its acute sector heartland as well as in long-stay and community services. As has been argued elsewhere (Wistow 1992c 1993), business planning in the NHS is founded upon implicit, if not explicit, assumptions about the availability of a wide range of services. Thus, early discharge from – as well as inappropriate admissions and re-admissions to – acute beds is influenced by the adequacy of health and social care services outside hospitals. The ability to meet waiting list targets is similarly affected by throughput and discharge rates. Over the past decade, the social security system has provided a 'fast track' procedure for hospital discharges. However, the funding changes since April 1993 have effectively transferred control over those discharges to social services departments. Thus, the way in which the latter exercise their new purchasing power and the skill with which they manage the new social care market are factors of profound concern to purchasers and providers in the NHS as well as to the Management Executive.

It was a growing appreciation of this fundamental interdependence between the health and social care markets that led to the publication of the joint Management Executive and Social Services Inspectorate guidance on achieving a smooth transition, to which we referred in Chapter 1. A central feature of that guidance was that social services departments should regard the 1992/93 broad pattern of social security funding as an 'implied commitment' for 1993/94 (Department of Health 1992b, c). As in the first year of the NHS internal market, therefore, the aim was to achieve something close to 'steady state' while authorities developed necessary understandings and expertise in market management. The switch to needs-led and community-based services took second place to more prosaic, if no less legitimate, immediate imperatives to safeguard the interests of existing users, independent sector suppliers and the NHS.

This definition of the initial tasks for social services departments had still to be defined by the Department of Health when we conducted our fieldwork in 1991. Indeed, subsequent chapters reveal how far most of them would have to travel before they identified and accepted such a role. Thus, the study on which this book is based throws light on the ways in which social services departments were initially interpreting and preparing to meet the demands of both developing and managing what most of them still understand as a mixed economy rather than a market of social care. In so doing, however, it highlights the importance of preparing for a process of managed change over a number of years. If the end point which authorities are expected to reach amounts to a radical transformation in service systems, the incrementalism of the Foster/ Laming letters may appear prudent and desirable.

Before presenting our empirical data on the initial stages of implementing change, we present evidence on what is effectively the collective starting point for that process of implementation in terms of the service and funding base for social care in 1991.

3

The mixed economy in 1991

Community care

The mixed economy of social care is not a new phenomenon. The public
sector has never been the sole provider or funder of social welfare services.
In fact, most social care is provided by the informal sector, and of course the
voluntary and private sectors are the mainstays of parts of social services
provision in some areas of the country. Within the public sector there are
many service provider and funding bodies, with numerous and often complex
links between them. The government's policy aim for community care, therefore, has been to encourage the *further* mixing of an already pluralist social
care economy.

What was the starting point for local authorities as, in April 1991, they
implemented the first round of reforms introduced by the 1990 Act? What
did the mixed economy of care look like? This chapter describes the funding
and provision of key social care services in 1991, illustrating that a mixed
economy already existed in England (our figures deal only with England),
although its past course of development had often been unplanned, indeed
sometimes the creation of perverse incentives. We first introduce a simple
framework which links provider and purchaser activities, and also highlights
some of the key policy options for the organization and funding of care. We
then describe the comparative underdevelopment of a mixed economy by
offering three illustrations: local authority funding of the voluntary and private
sectors; the supply of residential care for elderly people and its multiple sources

of funding; and the provision and funding of support and care services for elderly people with dementia.

The mixed economy of care

In its broadest interpretation, encouragement of a mixed economy could take the form of any relaxing of central or local government control or influence over the three dimensions of provision, funding and regulation (Knapp 1989).

Provision

At its simplest, the provider or supply side of the mixed economy comprises four main sectors:

- The *public sector* includes local authorities, with their social care, education, leisure, recreation and library responsibilities; the National Health Service, with its separate purchaser and provider units, and including family health services authorities; and the Department of Social Security. Social services authorities are of course the pivotal agents of the new community care system.
- The *voluntary sector* comprises all those formal organizations independent of government which, although they may earn profits, are bound by the 'non-distribution constraint' and cannot distribute those profits to any owners or share-holders (Kendall and Knapp 1993). Many but by no means all voluntary organizations have charitable status, conferring certain tax advantages and ensuring Charity Commission oversight.
- The *private sector* is obviously not bound by the non-distribution constraint. It is profit-seeking and distributing, and constitutionally separate from government. In recent years, the private sector has become a much more important provider of social services.
- The *informal or household sector* is the fourth main provider group. It comprises a large number of individual carers (family members, neighbours and others) and some small groups of carers, but the groups have no formal constitution or set of rules.

The boundaries between these sectors are blurred. Some private agencies disguise themselves as voluntary; some voluntary agencies behave in a manner fully consistent with maximization of either profits or managers' salaries; and a growing number of public agencies are developing many of the trappings of commercial enterprises, or are establishing not-for-profit trusts to run certain services under contract. Not surprisingly, there is debate and occasional controversy about how to draw the lines and distinctions between the sectors.

This categorization of provider types is the minimum needed for a discussion of England's mixed economy. In our interviews with local authority directors and members, they mentioned and compared a wider variety of

Box 3.1 Provider options

A. continuing local authority provision as organized in 1991, with no planned changes to the management, funding or regulation of activities;

B. continuing local authority provision with reorganization of the social services department along the lines of a purchaser/provider split of some kind and to some degree;

C. management or staff buy-outs of some local authority services;

D. floating off some services to not-for-profit trusts, allowing the authority to retain some degree of control, though with eligibility for DSS payments;

E. selling services, perhaps at a nominal price, to voluntary organizations (new or already working in the authority) which act independently of the authority, except for any service agreements or contracts;

F. selling services to private (for-profit) agencies (new or already with a presence in the authority) which act independently of the authority, except for any service agreements or contracts;

G. encouraging (or perhaps simply not stopping) voluntary or not-for-profit organizations setting up new services;

H. encouraging (or perhaps simply not stopping) private (for-profit) agencies setting up new services;

I. considering health authorities as potential providers of some social care services, such as residential care for elderly people or people with mental health problems; and

J. bringing NHS trusts into the supply picture.

provider options (Box 3.1). These ten options are not mutually exclusive, but there were some clear and largely predictable local priority rankings among them. Rarely were any two authorities alike, so it would be wrong to generalize too freely, but most Labour authorities preferred D to E, and strongly preferred E to F. Indeed, option F was a non-starter in some authorities. If the possibility was mentioned, they also ruled out J and were often unhappy about H. To take another example, most Conservative authorities supported option G, expressed some practical but not ideological reservations about H, and usually liked the idea of E and F in principle even though elected members had some difficulty supporting the sale of facilities in their own wards. Option C hardly ever received support from either officers or members, and it was too early for local authorities to make any judgements about the viability of option J.

These are gross generalizations, and the local reality was always far more interesting. Indeed, one of the strong conclusions to emerge from our contacts with a large number of authorities is that generalizations along party political lines are often hard to sustain. Some of these supply options will be considered in Chapters 4 to 7 (and see Hoggett and Taylor 1993 for a different way to group provider types). Although inadequate for discussion of some of the supply arrangements that have emerged and are still emerging in social care, our simple four-fold categorization of supply as public, voluntary, private or informal describes the level of aggregation used in routinely available social care statistics.

Purchasing

Along the purchasing or demand dimension of the mixed economy are arranged numerous sources of revenue, between them indicating who pays for a service, consumer, tax payer or donor. Six principal demand or funding routes can be distinguished.

- *Coerced collective demand* – where the public sector acts as purchaser on behalf of citizens, mandated by the electoral process. Funding comes predominantly from (coercive) taxation. Social services departments, for example, are funded from the general revenue support grant distributed by central government, specific grants from central government to fund particular services or functions (for example, social care services for people who are mentally ill and the training of social services staff), locally raised revenues from the council tax and business rates, and fees and charges for services.
- *Uncoerced or voluntary collective demand* – where voluntary organizations (and occasionally other bodies) use voluntarily donated funds to purchase services. The choice as to precisely what goods or services to purchase, and for precisely whom, is controlled by the organization and not (directly) by individual donors.
- *Corporate demand* – funding or support in kind from private sector corporations or firms.
- *Uncompensated individual consumption* – payment for goods or services consumed by the payer, but not subsidized from social security or other transfer payments.
- *Compensated individual consumption* – also payment for consumption by the payer, but now subsidized from transfer payments such as social security and housing benefit. A number of social security benefits contribute towards enabling people to live in domestic rather than residential settings. Both the number of benefits and the conditions governing eligibility for their receipt make for complexity. Benefits which directly contribute to community living include attendance allowance, invalid care allowance, mobility allowance and Social Fund community care grants. Benefits which contribute indirectly include means-tested income support and various specialist

benefits for people with physical disabilities or chronic illness (such as the contributory, non-means-tested invalidity allowance and the non-contributory, non-means-tested severe disablement and attendance allowances).

- *Individual donation* – payment for goods and services to be consumed by someone else, payments being made directly to suppliers and not to voluntary organizations as intermediary bodies (the latter being uncoerced collective demand).

In some cases the term 'payment' can be used as a shorthand for the transfer of goods or time, as well as money. Many social care services are funded from more than one source, and certainly most of the multi-service 'packages' of care used by people with greater needs for support will be funded directly from a variety of these sources. Some sources are mutually exclusive, by virtue of their eligibility criteria.

Regulation

Regulation is the third dimension of a mixed economy sometimes distinguished in broader discussions of privatization. An amount of public sector influence is exercised over the activities of social services providers indirectly, for example through tax policies as they affect corporations and charities, and through hegemonic influence in setting professional training curricula and, to a degree, broad public expectations of service availability and orientation. Rather more direct in their influences are three main types of regulatory action:

- Regulation is performed by central government through its legislative, executive and judicial branches (the last of these assuming increasing importance through the process of judicial review). The 1990 Act gave the Department of Health new powers to call for reports and issue directives. Much of the regulation is operationalized through the *Social Services Inspectorate*, an arm of the Department of Health.
- At local level are the new arm's-length *inspection units* introduced by the 1990 Act. These units are part of the local authority, but may not remain part of the social services department, and are charged with the responsibility of inspecting *all* provision, whether private, voluntary or public, and making their reports widely available. Guidance from the Department of Health has added lay members to these units' advisory committees, and encouraged global as well as facility inspections. Statutory complaints procedures reinforce these local regulatory powers.
- Third, there is regulation via contracting, whether through the formal, legally binding contracts drawn up by local authority purchasers with non-statutory or statutory sector providers, or through less formalized and generally less specific grant aid. Contracts may be agreed at the authority level or by case managers working with individual service users and their families.

There is currently also discussion of increased self-regulation through the establishment of a General Services Council, which could introduce codes of practice governing professional standards.

The mixed economy matrix

There are some potentially persuasive reasons for maintaining a distinction between the supply and funding dimensions when seeking to develop a mixed economy of social care and to massage it into good shape through local policy initiatives (see Chapter 5). Among the arguments for separation voiced by local authorities are clarification of fundamental objectives and reduction of provider vested interests, while central government has stressed the benefits for supply-side competition. There are also analytical and didactic benefits for separating the principles of purchasing and providing. For example, policy rationales behind supply-side subsidies to the voluntary sector – such as tax exemptions, grants or purchase of service contracts – are different in origin and implication from the rationales behind demand-side subsidies to consumers of voluntary sector services, such as income support payments or vouchers.

Cross-classifying the provider and purchaser dimensions produces a simple and informative representation of a pluralist welfare system. The resultant 24-celled matrix is a stylized description of the myriad interrelationships between demand and supply within a mixed economy, illustrated by the configurations of services in Figure 3.1. It is interesting to observe that every cell of the matrix can be filled with examples of social care provision and funding predating implementation of the 1990 Act. The mixed economy *before* the Act already contained an array of transaction types which the new legislation seeks to develop and expand.

Easily the two most important of the policy changes now in train are the promotion of market forces and the use of contracts by public authorities to purchase services from the private and voluntary sectors (and from other parts of the public sector), both representing changes in the mixed economy of *supply*. Each of these was addressed during our interviews with local authority and other personnel, and each is considered in some detail in subsequent chapters.[1] A contrary policy shift – one which diminishes the mixed economy of *purchasing* – is the rerouting of the funding of residential and nursing home care from demand-side to supply-side subsidies (and via local government rather than the Department of Social Security) from April 1993. This is a shift from purchasing through compensated individual consumption to coerced collective demand, though the source of funding (public expenditure) remains the same, since we do not operate a true insurance system. Employing this representation of the mixed economy we can define *privatization* as any move from the first row downwards (a reduction in direct, tax-based public expenditure) or from the first column to the right (delegation of service provision to non-public agencies via contracting-out or other means, or to individuals by passive neglect or active support of family and other carers). In addition,

Figure 3.1 The mixed economy matrix: social care examples

Purchase, demand or funding	*Provision or supply of services*			
	Public sector	*Voluntary sector*	*Private sector*	*Informal sector*
Coerced collective demand	Local authority field social work services	Contracted-out day care	Publicly funded placements in private residential homes	Foster family care for children funded by SSD
Uncoerced or voluntary collective demand	Voluntary organization payments for public sector training programmes	Self-help group paying for expert advice from larger voluntary organization	Purchases of goods and services by Mind or Age Concern	Foster family placements arranged and funded by Barnardo's
Corporate demand	Private residential home payments for LA registration and inspection	Corporate donations to charities	Private nursing home purchases of food, electricity, etc.	Employers' payments for employees' childminding
Uncompensated individual consumption	User charges for LA home help support	Parental payments for pre-school day care	Payment for private residential care by family or resident	Private childminder services
Compensated individual consumption	LA residential home fees backed up by pensions	Board and lodging payments to voluntary homes	Housing benefit and other user subsidies for private housing	Purchases from community care grants
Individual donation (for use by others)	Volunteers working in LA intermediate treatment unit	Donations to the Children's Society or Mencap	Volunteers in private residential homes	Intra-family transfers of resources and care

a third form of privatization – *deregulation* (any relaxing of public control over either production or funding) – can be superimposed. However, deregulation has not been a feature of the social services sector in recent years.

It is not our intention to attempt a comprehensive statistical or narrative description of the mixed economy of care at the start of the 1990s. Any such attempt would be frustrated by the current paucity of available statistics: those statistics routinely collected by government agencies do not span the full range of social care provision, and specially commissioned research studies have not yet been able to paint a national picture. Instead, we focus on three areas, each of them clearly illustrating that a mixed economy of care was already quite well established in Britain at the start of the decade (that is, before the implementation of the 1990 Act), but that it was likely to undergo radical change before the decade was out. The next section summarizes local authority expenditure on services provided by the voluntary and private sectors; we go on to examine the provision and funding of residential care for elderly people, the largest of the social care services; and the final section concentrates on elderly people with dementia, a client group whose care is certain to account for an increasingly large proportion of public and private funding over at least the next few decades.

Local authority funding of the independent sectors

Local authority funding of private and voluntary sector provision has a long pedigree, although it has been comparatively rare to find an authority con- tracting out as large a proportion of its statutory responsibilities as is today being contemplated, and indeed implemented, in some parts of the country. The ready availability of income support payments by the Department of Social Security was the primary reason for the explosion of private and (to a lesser extent) voluntary residential and nursing home provision during the 1980s. But local authorities themselves have also been important funders of non-statutory provision.

This is clear from the statistics gathered on the annual revenue return submitted by local authorities to central government. The RO3 statistics distinguish three routes by which local authority social services departments provide financial support for the non-statutory sectors:

- payments to voluntary organizations (the figures for English authorities in 1990/91, the year before implementation of the 1990 NHS and Community Care Act, are summarized in Table 3.1);
- payments to private organizations and private registered persons (Table 3.2); and
- general contributions to voluntary organizations (Table 3.3).

It will be obvious from our earlier discussion that these financial transfers do not represent the sum of local authority support for the non-statutory

Table 3.1 Local authority expenditure, England, 1990/91: payments to voluntary organizations

Service type and client group	Payments to voluntary organizations as a percentage of total expenditure on the corresponding service and client group				
	Inner London	Outer London	Metropolitan districts	Shire counties	All authorities
Residential care					
Elderly	13.7	2.7	0.5	0.4	2.2
Younger physically disabled	28.2	63.2	32.9	38.9	40.3
Mentally ill	8.8	33.3	1.4	16.0	14.1
Adults with learning disabilities	25.0	30.5	6.0	17.4	16.8
Children with learning disabilities	19.2	20.3	11.7	9.5	12.8
Other children	13.6	9.4	10.2	6.6	8.9
Mixed client groups	0.0	14.9	0.0	0.0	1.6
Non-residential care					
Elderly	1.2	1.4	0.5	1.1	1.0
Younger physically disabled	3.3	11.1	6.4	9.7	8.0
Mentally ill	0.2	3.7	0.7	4.5	2.8
Adults with learning disabilities	2.4	5.0	1.0	1.6	2.1
Children	0.7	2.8	4.2	4.9	3.9
Mixed client groups	0.4	0.0	3.0	1.8	1.7
All services, all client groups	4.5	5.6	2.7	3.5	3.5

Source: Local authority RO3 returns (PSS General Fund Revenue Account, 1990/91).

sectors, for there are non-financial means of support (such as staff secondments or rent-free facilities) as well as grants or other payments from other local authority departments such as housing or education, and indirect subsidies in the form of partial or total exemption from business rates. Other parts of the public sector provide support either directly, for example through NHS purchases of private nursing home services and Housing Corporation grants to housing associations, or indirectly in the form of tax exemptions for charities. The RO3 statistics can therefore paint only an incomplete picture even of local authority support for the private and voluntary sectors. Moreover, during our analyses we uncovered a number of data anomalies which we corrected or side-stepped by excluding authorities from the summary descriptions, but there will undoubtedly remain errors in the statistics which are not so obvious.

Table 3.2   Local authority expenditure, England, 1990/91: payments to private organizations

Service type and client group	Payments to private organizations as a percentage of total LA expenditure on the corresponding service and client group				
	Inner London	Outer London	Metropolitan districts	Shire counties	All authorities
Residential care					
Elderly	3.1	2.0	2.5	0.1	1.6
Younger physically disabled	0.8	4.2	1.2	5.6	3.3
Mentally ill	3.6	7.5	3.3	6.6	5.2
Adults with learning disabilities	9.1	9.3	1.3	5.1	4.9
Children with learning disabilities	8.7	10.8	3.4	3.0	5.0
Other children	6.5	9.7	2.6	2.8	4.3
Mixed client groups	0.8	0.0	0.0	16.7	5.0
Non-residential care					
Elderly	0.0	0.2	0.4	0.5	0.3
Younger physically disabled	0.0	1.4	0.1	1.8	0.9
Mentally ill	0.0	0.0	0.0	1.1	0.4
Adults with learning disabilities	0.1	0.1	0.3	0.2	0.2
Children	1.5	9.9	3.6	2.1	3.9
Mixed client groups	0.0	0.0	0.0	0.3	0.1
All services, all client groups	2.2	3.2	1.2	1.0	1.5

Source: Local authority RO3 returns (PSS General Fund Revenue Account, 1990/91).

Despite these difficulties, the figures in Tables 3.1 to 3.3 reveal the broad orders of magnitude of local authority social services department funding of private and voluntary organizations in 1990/91. It is clear that social services departments spent only small proportions in 'payments' (which are mainly contracts of one form or another, although relatively few of our sample authorities used this term in 1991 for these transfers) and in general contributions (grants). Aggregating the three forms of financial transfer gives the percentages in Table 3.4. Averaged across all client groups and services, these various payments and contributions amounted to just over 6 per cent of total social services spending at the start of the decade. This compares with 8 per cent in 1978/79 (Judge and Smith 1983) and 6 per cent in 1988/89.

Table 3.3   Local authority expenditure, England, 1990/91: general contributions to voluntary organizations

| Service type and client group | General contributions to voluntary organizations as a percentage of total LA expenditure on the corresponding service and client group | | | | |
	Inner London	Outer London	Metropolitan districts	Shire counties	All authorities
Elderly	0.9	1.1	0.5	0.8	0.7
Younger physically disabled	2.5	11.4	4.0	4.4	5.3
Mentally ill	1.3	4.2	4.5	7.9	5.4
Adults with learning disabilities	1.3	0.7	0.8	0.7	0.8
Children	2.5	1.8	1.5	1.5	1.6
Mixed client group	15.8	9.4	5.1	9.2	8.4
All client groups	2.6	1.5	1.2	1.4	1.4

Source: Local authority RO3 returns (PSS General Fund Revenue Account, 1990/91).

Table 3.4   Local authority expenditure, England, 1990/91: funding of the private and voluntary sectors (all payment types)

| Service type and client group | Funding of private and voluntary sectors as a percentage of total LA expenditure on the corresponding service and client group | | | | |
	Inner London	Outer London	Metropolitan districts	Shire counties	All authorities
Elderly people	9.1	4.2	2.5	1.5	3.0
Younger physically disabled adults	14.0	35.1	20.3	35.3	27.5
Mentally ill people	8.1	23.3	10.2	20.7	16.3
Adults with learning disabilities	27.5	24.6	5.3	11.7	16.3
Children	15.9	19.8	11.8	10.6	13.1
Mixed client group	16.7	12.2	8.6	11.7	11.1
All client groups[a]	8.4	10.3	5.1	5.4	6.4

Note:
[a]   The denominator includes local authority spending on PSS support services (fieldwork, training, administration).
Source: Local authority RO3 returns (PSS General Fund Revenue Account, 1990/91).

Not surprisingly given the uneven development of private and voluntary services and the differences between authorities in their attitudes to these other sectors, this overall national average hides considerable variation. For example, summing the relevant percentages in Tables 3.1 to 3.3, we find that 44 per cent of identified SSD expenditure on residential services for adults with physical disabilities was allocated to the non-statutory sectors, compared to only 4 per cent of local spending on residential care for elderly people. Table 3.4 reveals other client group differences. Comparing Tables 3.1 and 3.2, it can be seen that authorities supported the voluntary sector more than the private, and comparing Tables 3.1 and 3.3 it is clear that payments via contracts amounted to larger sums than transfers in the form of grants. London boroughs contracted out much higher proportions of their services than metropolitan districts and shire counties. In Inner London, 8.4 per cent of total social services expenditure went to the voluntary and private sectors in 1990/91, compared to 10.3 per cent in Outer London, 5.1 per cent in the metropolitan districts and 5.4 per cent in the shire counties.

These expenditure data were also examined in relation to political control, measured in terms of the number of seats held by each party in May 1989, this being relevant to budgetary decisions in 1990/91. Conservative-controlled authorities had a greater propensity to contract out than authorities controlled by the other parties or with hung councils, but there appeared to be no relationship between political control and grant-giving.[2] Our interviews indicated that attitudes to funding the non-statutory sectors were clearly conditioned by political opinions concerning the legitimate roles of local government. For example, the Labour Chair of social services in one of our sample authorities expressed reluctance to reduce the direct service provision of the authority, saying 'We prefer to think that we are doers rather than managers: activating things and getting things organized and running, rather than just like a pre-scription clerk when you go to the doctor's.'

However, there is some evidence that the differences in purchasing policy are narrowing, with Labour authorities increasing the proportion of social services spending in the form of contract payments and grants between 1987/88 and 1990/91, while there was no marked change in Conservative authorities. This may have reflected a change in attitudes or a response to financial constraints within Labour authorities. It would, of course, be naive to examine only two dimensions (authority type and political control) when attempting to unravel the pattern of local authority funding of the non-statutory sectors. Our interviews revealed a more complex pattern of determinants, as have previous statistical enquiries (Judge and Smith 1983; Knapp 1986).

Fiscal pressures were said to be playing an important part. Many of our local authority interviewees described how the ability to develop an 'enabling role' as envisaged in the 1989 White Paper was conditioned by financial constraints. Difficulties had been caused or exacerbated by spending restrictions and revenue support grant cuts. It was argued by a number of interviewees, for example, that community charge (poll tax) limits followed by capping had forced substantial cuts to the grants budget, and voluntary sector representatives told us of numerous grants which had been axed and distinctive contributions which had been lost. Local authority budget restrictions also provided the incentive to reduce direct service provision and to increase purchases from the non-statutory sectors in order to meet statutory obligations. The relatively low cost (whether real or imagined) of the non-statutory sectors was attractive. A general move away from comparatively loose grant arrangements towards contracts had often pre-dated the 1990 Act (see Chapter 5).

Another influence on local authority spending patterns was the existing level, orientation and quality of non-statutory sector provision. In one authority the small scale of grant support was rationalized by the small number and size of voluntary organizations, the Director describing the sector as 'under-developed', although he admitted that little had been done to assist its growth or consolidation. In another authority, the voluntary sector was small but seen as strong because of its independence: 'it manages without [local authority funding] so we leave it at that'. In authorities which professed closer adherence to Clarke and Stewart's (1990) vision of enabling as community governance (see Chapter 2), there was an enduring commitment to continued grant aid. The staff of one London borough, for example, told us that grant aid to voluntary organizations had traditionally been substantial. The sector was lively and contained a number of active groups in the sphere of campaigning and advocacy as well as provision. Work with ethnic minorities and women was particularly strong. The authority was planning to continue to support the sector with grants.

The potential future contribution of the voluntary sector to residential care provision was generally thought to be more limited than that of the private sector, although housing associations were often mentioned as important vehicles for expansion. The voluntary sector made a greater contribution than the private sector to day care, domiciliary support, self-help and other non-residential services. Many local authority interviewees saw day care (specialist and other) as the voluntary sector's major service provider role, and many made grants or agreed contracts in support of it. Services for people from ethnic minorities were a speciality of the sector in some areas, and the flexibility and small scale of operation of many organizations were also seen as beneficial. Campaigning and advocacy activities were identified by many local authority officers and members as distinctive, perhaps unique, but not so valuable as to be indispensable in times of local authority financial hardship, particularly if they were seen to be at odds with direct service provision. As we describe in Chapter 6, growth in service provision, especially under contract to the public sector, threatens to compromise a number of traditional voluntary sector objectives and to damage some of its widely recognized virtues, such as flexibility, participative styles of management, specialization, variety and independence.

The private sector's main contribution was residential care provision, with other areas of activity reported to be relatively underdeveloped, although many local authority interviewees saw potential for new roles. A few people described the beginnings of private sector diversification into day and domiciliary care. Some proprietors had begun to offer day care within residential establishments, and some were using their establishments as bases for domiciliary services, but developments were reportedly few and slow. Some local authority interviewees mentioned local private domiciliary care agencies which existed quite independently of residential provision. However, most officers admitted that they knew little about the small-scale, informal and often new activities of the private sector, so that the extent of the sector's non-residential provision could be a lot larger than generally assumed.

Residential care provision and funding

The biggest change in the mixed economy in recent years has been the huge expansion of private sector residential and nursing home care. This is widely interpreted as an unintended consequence of what was said to be simply clarification and subsequently equalization of social security funding entitlements. This made it possible for elderly and other adults to obtain ready access to non-statutory homes without assessment of their care needs. The combined effects of this liberal social security regime and the fiscal constraints on local government can be seen in relation to market shares in the largest of the residential care sectors – supporting elderly people and younger adults with physical disabilities (Figure 3.2).

It is not clear how far the availability of social security payments, subject to a financial means test, merely funded a latent preference among elderly people and their families for independent rather than public sector provision. Identification with a particular religious or ethnic group, for example, has always generated a demand for voluntary sector services, and there were as many as 25,000 elderly people in private sector homes in 1975, but during the 1980s the preference for private sector care grew rapidly. The marked growth in the number and value of occupational pensions, and higher levels of disposable income generally, coupled with modest and more recent growth in long-term care insurance and 'equity release schemes', may give future generations of elderly people the economic ability to satisfy preferences for private sector care, but for the current generation of actual and potential users of residential care it was certainly the entitlement of many of them to social security funding which exerted the greatest influence. As one Director of Social Services put it:

> In 1979 there were five private homes in the county and now there are ninety-four, so you can see that ever since Rhodes Boyson [then a Minister at the Department of Health and Social Security] made his famous mistake about opening up the social security system...there has been a huge mushrooming of residential homes in the private sector.

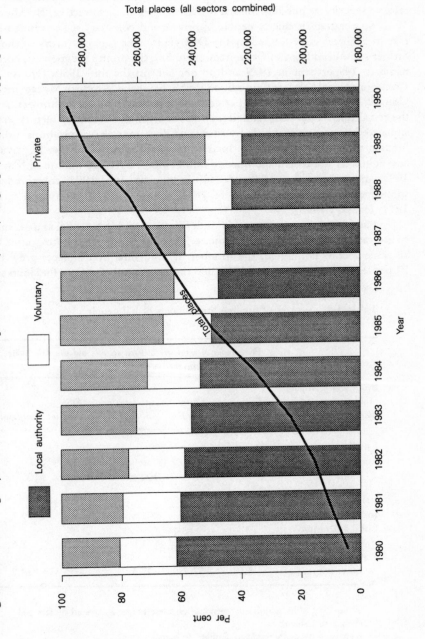

Figure 3.2. Percentage by sector and total residential places for elderly and younger physically handicapped people

Many people who could probably have managed well in the community with a modest amount of home care support found the financial advantages and relative security of publicly funded residential care to be attractive. By March 1991, 60 per cent of elderly people in private and voluntary sector residential care in England were funded by the DSS via income support (many of them further subsidized from other sources, including the homes themselves), compared to 14 per cent in 1979 and 36 per cent in the mid-1980s (House of Commons Social Services Committee 1985b; Ernst and Whinney Management Consultants 1986). Another 2 per cent were funded by local authorities, and the remaining 39 per cent funded themselves or (in the voluntary sector) were supported in part or in whole by charitable donations or organizations' other income sources (see Table 3.5). Income support payments for care in private and voluntary residential and nursing homes totalled £1,300 million in March 1991, and perhaps as much as £2,480 million by April 1993, compared to supplementary benefit payments of £10 million in 1979 (Henwood *et al.* 1991; Hansard 1993).

The growth in the demand for independent sector residential and nursing home care during the 1980s was met with a mixed supply-side response. In all three sectors combined, the number of residential home places grew by 57 per cent between 1980 and 1991, and there was an almost four-fold increase

Table 3.5   Sources of funding for residents of old people's homes, England, March 1991

Sector and principal funding source and client group	Percentages of residents in each sector's old people's homes funded from different sources				
	Inner London	Outer London	Metropolitan districts	Shire counties	All authorities
Local authority homes					
Local authority funding[a]	100	100	100	100	100
Private and voluntary homes					
Income support[b]	66.2	59.0	71.5	56.8	59.7
Local authority contracts[b]	25.3	8.4	1.0	0.5	1.6
Private means and other sources[c]	8.5	32.7	27.5	42.6	38.7

Notes:
[a]   27 per cent of local authority spending on these homes is covered by fees and charges to residents.
[b]   Includes top-ups by residents, families or homes.
[c]   Privately funded or funded from organizations' own income (charitable donations, investments).

in the number of nursing home places. The costs of setting up a home were relatively low – for example, in many areas of the country there was a low-priced supply of suitable premises (small guesthouses and former hotels), and banks and other financial institutions were willing to make loans – and not obviously different between the voluntary and private sectors. Yet the private sector grew rapidly during the 1980s and the voluntary sector did not. The number of private residential home places grew by 334 per cent between 1980 and 1991, and its market share increased from 19 to 54 per cent. In contrast, the voluntary sector's market share fell from 19 to 13 per cent over the same period, even though the number of voluntary home places was 5 per cent larger.[3] Although voluntary organizations have the comparative advantage of tax exemptions and access to donative capital, they do not appear to benefit from a greater supply of volunteer or low-wage staff. Few voluntary home workers are unpaid; Ernst and Whinney (1986) put the figure at less than 3 per cent and identified no systematic differences in hiring practices between voluntary and private homes. The private sector can raise the equity capital necessary to finance new ventures by offering the prospect of dividends to investors, while the voluntary sector is legally bound by the constraint that it can earn but not distribute profits. There has emerged a new entrepreneurial class prepared to make considerable investments in the private residential care market (Bradshaw 1988), while the voluntary sector appeared not to be interested in expansion in this particular market (Forder and Knapp 1993a).

By 1988, the private sector had displaced local government as the largest provider in the residential care sector. There were higher proportions of independent home places, especially in the private sector, in authorities where Conservatives were in the majority or the largest grouping, although recently there has been a relative rise in the private sector's market share in Labour authorities.[4] Across our sample, we found no association between political control and the proportion of total places in the voluntary sector. However, as we cautioned when describing the correlation between local authority spending patterns and political control, the underlying associations are complex and mediated through a host of other influential factors (Forder and Knapp 1993b). For example, the relative economic prosperity of an area is likely to influence both voting patterns and the attractiveness of private sector investment, and our local authority and independent sector interviewees posited a number of other economic and geographical factors which help to explain the intersectoral balance of provision. In Inner London, the relatively low provision by the private sector and high provision by the voluntary sector were seen to be the result of the combination of inner-city deprivation and high prices, which made the area less financially attractive for the private sector. There was also a long-standing tradition of voluntary action. A county Director attributed the low private sector provision in his area to relatively high capital and labour costs and the lack of a coastal strip. Another Director saw the development of voluntary action as arising from what he termed the 'culture of deprivation' following the decline of traditional local industries.

Another characterized the local voluntary sector as 'small and patchy', partly because the county had no large towns, and 'therefore every small town has its own branch of everything'.

Client group illustration – elderly people with dementia

Another way to illustrate the multiplicity of providers and funding arrangements within the mixed economy – and our final example – is to focus on a single client group. Elderly people with dementia have needs for many social care and other services, and their numbers will increase over the next three decades or more. Using survey data collected by the Office of Population Censuses

Table 3.6 Elderly people with advanced cognitive impairment, England: estimated prevalence in 1991 and funding responsibilities under new arrangements (post April 1993)

Place of accommodation	Estimated prevalence[a] (000)	Average weekly cost (1991/92 price levels)				
		Total (£)	DHA (%)	FHSA (%)	LA SSD (%)	User/ family/ DSS (%)
Private household, living alone	42.8	207	8.0	1.4	12.4	78.2[b]
Private household, living with others	159.7	237	13.2	1.3	8.0	77.5[c]
Local authority residential home	45.2	319	2.3	2.3	92.1	3.3
Private or voluntary residential home	15.1	223	2.2	2.2	27.3	68.2[d]
Private or voluntary nursing home	23.3	321	2.3	2.3	42.5	52.9[d]
Hospital	33.8	729	95.7	0.0	2.9	1.4

Notes:
[a] Number of elderly people with advanced cognitive impairment (dementia) as defined from the OPCS scale of intellectual impairment. See source for details.
[b] Of which, it is estimated that 29 per cent is the opportunity cost of informal care, 45 per cent is personal consumption cost and 26 per cent is accommodation cost. The proportions met by users, families and DSS cannot be reliably estimated at the national level.
[c] Of which, it is estimated that 36 per cent is the opportunity cost of informal care, 41 per cent is personal consumption cost and 23 per cent is accommodation costs. The proportions met by users, families and DSS cannot be reliably estimated at the national level.
[d] Some part of this cost may be met from the charitable and other independent income sources of voluntary homes.
Source: Kavanagh et al. (1993).

and Surveys in 1985 and 1986, supplemented with evidence from PSSRU research studies, Kavanagh *et al.* (1993) estimated the prevalence of 'cognitive impairment'[5] among elderly people in 1991, their places of residence, the support services received and the associated costs. We can use this combination of data to illustrate both the mixed economy of funding and the impact of the funding responsibility reforms introduced in April 1993. Thus Table 3.6 takes the service delivery arrangements of 1991 and attaches the new funding routes, revealing the importance of local authority funding within the emerging mixed economy. For example, comparison of the old and new responsibilities suggests that local authorities, which previously funded little of the cost of independent care homes, could be contributing 23 per cent of the funding of residential care homes and 43 per cent of the funding of nursing homes. This represents a significant leap in local authority purchasing power.

We can see therefore that the mixed economy of social care was already quite well developed in 1991, though there will clearly be marked changes during the 1990s. How local authorities reacted to those changes is the subject of the next chapter.

Notes

1   In this book we will not consider other policy options in the further development of the mixed economy, such as user charges for public sector services (see, for example, Knapp 1984: 99–107, for a discussion of historical context and principles; Netten 1993), the promotion of volunteering (see, for example, Shaw 1993), the encouragement of charitable donations, and the encouragement and support of informal care. We exclude these mainly for reasons of space, although the first has received little policy or research attention of late, and the second and third are arguably of limited *immediate* importance in the development of England's mixed economy of social care. The policy and practice issues and experiences concerning the fourth are comprehensively addressed in Allen and Perkins (1994).

2   Our analyses were simply the calculation of Pearson correlations. Multi-variate analyses which control for the full range of factors would offer a fairer test of this relationship.

3   The comparative growth of the private sector was not as marked in the supply of residential care for other client groups, where the voluntary sector has traditionally been regarded as a specialist and often exemplary provider, and where facilities need to employ experienced or professionally trained staff. For example, the private sector's share of the market for residential care of adults with learning disabilities grew from 10 per cent of all places in 1980 to 26 per cent in 1991 (or 480 per cent growth in the number of places), while the voluntary sector's share grew from 13 to 27 per cent (or 344 per cent growth in the number of places). In the residential care of adults with mental health problems, the private sector's share changed from 13 to 41 per cent, and the voluntary sector's from 23 to 24 per cent.

4   In Conservative-controlled councils there were no significant changes in the proportions of residential care places for elderly people in the non-statutory sectors between 1986 and 1991, although there was a significant fall in voluntary

sector market share in Conservative shire counties. The market share of the non-statutory sectors, particularly the private sector, grew significantly in Labour areas, although this was partly owing to Labour gaining control of authorities with higher levels of private provision.

5　The prevalence of dementia could not be estimated from the OPCS surveys, but the measure of cognitive impairment developed from the surveys' 'intellectual impairment' scales identifies dementia with sufficient accuracy for the broad purposes of our funding projections (see Kavanagh *et al.* 1993 for details).

4

Local responses to the legislation and guidance

Introduction

By any standards the change agenda for local authorities presented by the NHS and Community Care Act 1990 was enormous, and it required changes not merely to organizational structures and processes but also to the whole culture and ethos of social services departments. Moreover, the scale of organizational turbulence involved was increased further by the parallel implementation of the Children Act 1989, on the one hand, and the NHS changes, on the other.

In this chapter we outline authorities' initial responses to this change agenda. Our fieldwork sought to ascertain authorities' reactions to *Caring for People* and the NHS and Community Care Act both at a broad philosophical and political level and at the level of detailed organizational arrangements for implementation. In terms of the former, we wanted to establish, for example: whether local authorities supported the government's proposals because they reflected existing or developing local practice; whether they supported the White Paper's service philosophies and principles as well as the organizational principles it advocated (the enabling role and the mixed economy); and whether they were politically averse to stimulating some suppliers but not others. In the first of the two main sections of this chapter we draw especially upon the interviews with Directors and Chairs of social services to describe authorities' broad reactions to these aspects of the *Caring for People* implementation programme.

Broad reactions

Overall, we identified three notable general reactions from our interviewees: first, unanimous support for the service philosophy and principles enshrined in *Caring for People*; second, extreme anxiety about the availability of adequate resources to realize them; and third, caution about the main organizational principles – that is, the shift to an enabling role (in which enabling was seen as market development) and the requirement to promote a mixed economy of care. The most characteristic local response was simultaneously to endorse the development of predominantly non-residential services based on assessed individual need, and to be cautious or selective about the development of a mixed economy. As one Director commented, the government's proposals were 'welcomed in terms of service philosophy and direction' but there was, in his authority, 'an underlying anxiety that the whole thing raises expectations [which] you can't fulfil because you don't have enough money to develop the services further'.

Support for service philosophy and principles

Support for the White Paper's emphasis on needs-led and individualized services, and a shift wherever possible from residential to home-based care, was universal. Moreover, in many cases the government's proposals were said to have emerged from the field (see Wistow 1990b), and to reflect what had been the developing practice in authorities for some years, even prior to Griffiths: 'the government hasn't come up with anything new...a lot of the things we are either doing currently or planning to do'. In addition the Act's main features were said to be 'the kind of thing [we] have been doing for years'.

The most common view was that the government's aims and objectives represented a self-evident good. As one Director said, 'how could one disagree with the rhetoric of community care?' The common concern was not the direction being proposed but the reality of limited means and the nature of the organizational arrangements: 'the ideological stuff that's been inserted on the way about the mixed economy of care', as one interviewee put it.

This concern is addressed in the following sections. Here it is worth noting that the explicit, and unprompted, endorsement of the principle of user choice and independence was rarely matched by any comparable support for the other key White Paper principles of cost-effectiveness and value for money. Overwhelmingly, across twenty-four authorities embracing all political hues, the characteristic response to the legislative proposals was, on the one hand, support for the development of services aimed at maximizing user independence and carer support and, on the other, reservations about the enabling role as expressed in the legislation and about developing the mixed economy of care with any enthusiasm.

Caution and reservations

The general policy context

Local authorities' main priorities for change in late 1990 and early 1991 were to meet the 1 April 1991 deadline for establishing inspection units, complaints procedures and specific grant proposals. The implementation of the Children Act was also regarded as a more immediate priority than the development of a mixed economy. In addition to having these other priorities, authorities faced what they regarded as considerable political and policy uncertainties. First, there was uncertainty about whether the funding changes would be implemented in 1993. Second, there were doubts whether, after the general election, local authorities would continue to have the lead role, local government would be radically restructured and, especially in the event of a Labour government, there would be less emphasis on the mixed economy.

Compounding such political uncertainties, there was in virtually every authority considerable anxiety about the sheer lack of resources, whether capital or revenue, and about the absence – at that stage – of any ringfencing, as recommended by Griffiths. It is important to emphasize that such expressions of anxiety were voiced with equal strength across authorities, irrespective of political control. In one Conservative-controlled authority the Director spoke of the dilemma that existed because of the uncertainty about resources: 'this authority is not known for its altruistic approach to social services. It's that simple issue of uncertainty about resources. This council would be very pleased indeed to speed things up but it won't do so unless it can be certain of adequate resources.' The Chair of social services in this authority referred to the government's 'basic dishonesty' in, on the one hand, requiring authorities to provide services for people who have indeterminate needs and, on the other, distributing resources via the 'straightjacket' of standard spending assessments. In other Conservative-controlled councils there were similar complaints about 'the lack of clarity of funding'. One Director remarked that 'community care is fine as long as the money is there to provide proper community care' and, according to the Chair in another authority, 'the phrase "adequate funding" doesn't exactly fill us with a great deal of reassurance'. Serious concerns were also voiced about the lack of ringfencing: that even if adequate, resources might not actually come to social services departments.

Such concerns were also frequently expressed in authorities controlled by other political parties. According to one Labour Chair, 'we didn't mind taking on the extra role and the extra work as long as they gave us the wherewithal to do it. But they're not doing that and that's the main thing...they want us to do the job but they won't give us the money to do it.' In another Labour-controlled authority, it was said that 'the anxiety [was] whether it would be adequately and properly resourced: that without doubt was the major anxiety and always was'. In authorities threatened with, or already subject to, poll tax capping such anxieties were even more acute. Among London boroughs, there was extreme disappointment that 'there isn't the cash to back up some of the rhetoric' and, in another case, 'a definite feeling that the government is trying to get away with doing something on the cheap, leaving local authorities in the lurch with a poisoned chalice'. While not diminishing this widespread sense of anxiety, it is worth noting that we undertook fieldwork precisely when authorities were finalizing their budgets and when the prospect or fact of service reductions or cuts could be expected to be uppermost in interviewees' minds.

Interestingly, however, a corollary to this context of resource constraint was, it was acknowledged, that the development of a more mixed economy had become a simple necessity, since authorities would no longer be able to fund anything like previous or current levels of public provision. Acceptance of this necessity did not mean, however, that such a development would be pursued either enthusiastically or energetically.

Interpreting the legislation and guidance

Caring For People made clear the government's intention that social services authorities would be responsible for making 'maximum possible use of private and voluntary providers' (Secretaries of State 1989b: para. 1.11). It also identified ways in which authorities could promote the mixed economy, including 'taking steps to stimulate the setting up of "not for-profit" agencies', 'identifying areas of their own work which are sufficiently self-contained to be suitable for "floating off" as self-managed units'; and 'stimulating the development of new voluntary sector activity' (ibid.: para. 3.4.6, emphasis added).

The government's expectation, as expressed here, was that the local authority role should be an active not a passive one. Similarly, the Department of Health's subsequent policy guidance referred to local authorities 'seeking out' services from a range of providers (Department of Health 1990a: para. 4.3) and, more specifically, that

> where there is little existing choice in service provision or where a need has been identified for a service which is not available, SSDs should consider ways of encouraging these [and] develop strategies which will enable them to provide appropriate information and a supportive climate in order to encourage and facilitate the creation of new services by private and voluntary providers. (ibid.: para. 4.15)

By its nature, the term 'mixed economy' will mean different things in different local authority contexts, depending upon the nature of the existing service mix, the range of current and potential providers, and – as the policy guidance notes – the need to maintain 'stability in supply of care services for individuals' (ibid.: para. 4.11). There is in the policy guidance a tacit acceptance that, even if it wished, the government could not be prescriptive about the nature of the service mix in individual localities; about the proportion of services to be provided by voluntary, private or not-for-profit agencies; or, indeed, by statutory authorities. Two years later this attitude had changed. As indicated in Chapter 1, in 1992 the government decided to be highly prescriptive about the amount of transferred social security funds (85 per cent of the social security transfer) that local authorities should spend on independent sector services.

There was also in the policy guidance an explicit acceptance – echoing the point made by the SSI Chief Inspector in January 1990 (CI(90)3) – that in terms of the pace of development it would 'take several years rather than months' (Department of Health 1990b) to achieve a more mixed economy. Notwithstanding these original caveats about supply mix and speed of development, it was made clear that the government did expect local authorities to be actively stimulating a mixed economy of social care and that they would be looking for evidence of progress in this direction in authorities' first community care plans from 1 April 1993 (Department of Health 1990a: para. 2.25).

The evidence of our study, however, was that not all authorities regarded the active stimulation of a mixed economy as their job, let alone their priority. Many, indeed, were by contrast adopting a consciously passive stance. In only one authority (Conservative-controlled) was there an intention to examine all direct service provision in order to see, in the Chairman's words, 'whether it couldn't be better provided by somebody else, and at the same time looking at the possibilities for promoting competition'. More typical was the view of another Conservative Chair that the local authority could take a passive stance because a mixed economy 'is there around us. I don't think we have to take any steps...it doesn't need promoting. I think it will automatically promote itself.'

This latter view was characteristic of what could be described as the minimalist argument – expressed in many authorities, and irrespective of party control – that there is, and for many years has been, a mixed economy insofar as there is considerable private sector residential provision and/or significant voluntary sector day or domiciliary care. According to this view, authorities could legitimately say they were promoting a mixed economy merely by continuing their traditional support for voluntary organizations providing domiciliary care, for example, or by registering private residential homes. Such a view appears to fall some way short of what the government intended by 'active stimulation', however slowly this was undertaken.

Our fieldwork was planned to begin after authorities had received the policy guidance. In practice, the first four 'pilot' authorities had just received the document when we conducted the interviews and, by their own admission, the Directors concerned still had to absorb its contents. The remaining twenty Directors were asked whether the guidance assisted their authority's identification of priorities for change or affected its response to the Act. Two thought it too early to say whether the guidance would affect the authorities' priorities or response. A third authority was said to be 'ahead of the game' and, indeed, responsible – by example – for much of the guidance.

The other seventeen Directors can be roughly divided into two groups: fourteen who expressed their general approval and three who had some serious reservations. Among the former group, 'approval' typically meant that the guidance was clear and sensible. In fact seven of this group described the guidance as being useful. For example, it was described as 'extremely useful, we've used it as the straightforward meat of a lot of the work we've done'; as 'really quite well put together, [it] has influenced and focused more clearly some of the debates we've been having'; and as 'very useful: better than anything else that's come out in the way of guidance about any other legislation'. Among the remaining seven Directors, the guidance was generally described as 'fairly reasonable' and helpful in confirming the appropriateness of what they and their authorities were already considering and implementing.

Of the three Directors who expressed any serious reservations, one argued that the guidance was too removed from local authority practitioners. In the other two cases, the reservations were more significant and related to the status of the guidance. One Director remarked that it 'was not very clear what clout it has. And...that is a real problem in legal terms.' He contrasted this with the Children Act guidance, which was, he said, much more prescriptive. His view was that the community care guidance needed to be more specific, because it would be interpreted in widely different ways. The second of these two Directors voiced a similar concern, one which, he said, had arisen from the Rochdale child abuse case,

> where the definition of what is guidance and what is legislation and what you're required to do and what you can put aside is becoming more and more blurred and therefore people's anxieties are that if things do go wrong and you don't follow the guidance that you'll more or less then be told 'Well that's not guidance really, it is stronger than guidance'.

These latter calls for greater prescription and clarity represented a minority view across the sample authorities. By and large, the implicit view was that the legislation and guidance rightly allow scope for local interpretation – about what constitutes an appropriate service mix, what is the appropriate pace for development and what the enabling role entailed.

The implementation delay
The general reaction of local authority members and officers to the government's decision to phase in the legislative changes from 1991 to 1993 (see Chapter 1) comprised a mixture of anger at the reasons given for the delay, disappointment because of the adverse effects upon users, carers and staff, and an acceptance that more time would allow for better preparations for change.

As regards anger at the reasons given for delay, the views of interviewees across the twenty-four authorities were typified by the view of one Director that 'The reasons (the government) gave for it were totally spurious of course, nonsense really. They didn't want to because it would cost them a fortune and they were involved in the problems of the poll tax...any fool can see that.'

Another interviewee spoke of people being 'really very angry indeed' for a couple of months after the announcment. Thereafter, although the anger subsided, 'confidence in the government was not in any way restored...we just don't trust them, and nobody trusts them any longer'.

The widespread expressions of 'disappointment' about the delay had three main facets:

- the inability to proceed with planned developments without the resource transfers (and some doubts about whether these would be made as intended);
- the deleterious effect upon the morale of social services staff and upon users and carers; and
- the effect upon the ordering of priorities.

In the three authorities which professed themselves ready for the changes, disappointment was voiced about not being able to implement planned service developments. The Chair of one Conservative-controlled county council said there was 'an incredible sense of let-down and disappointment because we happened to be ready and raring to go, [but] until you get the transfers there is a limit to how much community care money we can use'. This same disappointment was echoed by the Chair of a Labour-controlled district council which could no longer proceed with 'a whole series of proposals which we'd brought forward [because] the extent to which we can go ahead with these, particularly those that have much costs attached to them, depend on the amount of money we've got'.

A small number of interviewees referred to the momentum that had built up within social services departments and the beneficial effect that a tight deadline had upon staff motivation. One Director suggested that the delay 'depressed morale' and it would be 'quite difficult to remotivate people to get them back into the frame of mind of enormous change'. Many more interviewees, however, spoke of the damaging effect of the delay upon the morale of users and carers. According to the Chair of one London borough:

there was a big peak of enthusiasm locally and then disillusionment that the money wasn't available, that the pace was slowing down in terms of central government and the Department of Health...that's been quite confusing for users of services and carers, that they'd read or heard that there was going to be this big change in community care, and it's still not quite happened.

Elsewhere it was argued that 'carers were left another two years to wait for all they were hoping for' and that, having had their expectations raised, their cynicism about the changes actually happening appeared justified. There was said to be 'a fear that it won't actually happen'.

In terms of effects upon local priorities, it was agreed in two authorities that the delay had been 'wholly negative' in 'having taken the pressure off both [local authority] members and health authorities', in which, consequently, community care 'had slipped down [the] agenda'.

The general view across the sample authorities was that they would have been ready to implement the legislative changes on 1 April 1991 as originally intended. The same view was expressed by authorities elsewhere. Surveys carried out prior to the delay announcement found that whereas 79 per cent of social services departments thought the 1 April 1991 deadline gave authorities insufficient lead time (Hatchett 1990), almost all authorities nevertheless expected to implement the reforms on schedule (*Social Services Insight*, 18 July 1990: 4).

It was widely conceded among the sample authorities that, if implementation was to be phased, authorities would be even better prepared.

> You can always use a change in time-scale to your advantage...and I'm sure some of the things will be better than they would have been if they'd been implemented together, [the delay] probably enabled us to look a little more carefully at what we're doing in the community care plans and that's a very good thing in itself.

According to one Chair, although there was 'enormous irritation at the time' the authority 'in organizational terms [would] benefit'. But, he added, 'I don't want you to think for a moment that I wasn't keen that we should go ahead with the implementation in the spring.'

In only three authorities was there said to be genuine relief at the delay. The Director of one Labour-controlled county council admitted to having 'made the right noises about how awful was the delay', but, he added, 'all of us breathed a sigh of relief privately saying, thank God, we'll have more time to put things in place'. The Director of another Labour-controlled shire county thought that 'it was absolutely the right decision to delay the introduction...it would have been absolutely disastrous to go ahead...we don't have the infrastructure which is competent to handle factors all of which are fast-moving and all of which are unpredictable.' Similarly, the Chair of one metropolitan district said that the reaction was 'absolute relief' because the authority 'would have been having a hell of a job trying to bring in that much change' from April 1991.

Few disagreed about this view of the scale of the task, although the majority maintained that their authority would have succeeded in meeting the April 1991 deadline. It is unquestionable, however, that the implementation delay was one of the main justifications for authorities adopting a slow and cautious approach to the development of a mixed economy. Such caution was, moreover, said to be amply justified by the Chief Social Services Inspector's letter in January 1990 setting out the establishment of inspection units, complaints procedures and proposals for specific grants as the main 1 April 1991 priorities. In addition, as indicated previously, the implementation of the Children Act appeared as a more immediate priority in some authorities.

Pride in public sector provision

A significant determinant of local authorities' willingness to diversify service provision will be their view of their own record in service provision as well as that of potential alternatives. In this respect, one striking feature was the extent to which local authority officers and members expressed a pride in public sector provision and a consequent concern about its enforced diminution. This was not an uncritical defence of all such provision, but a belief that the best of public sector provision would match the best of private or voluntary provision. What is more, this was the belief of all political parties. Thus, according to the Chair of a Conservative-controlled county, 'members of all parties feel a little apprehensive about handing over a service which has been perceived to be working extremely well to an untried management...that would be across the board, it doesn't matter what your politics are'.

Similarly, the Director of a Labour-controlled county said his members 'thought we were doing quite well the way we were' as service providers and preferred to think of themselves as 'doers rather than managers'. The Director in a Conservative-controlled county similarly referred to 'leading politicians [who] see the public sector provision as very important...there is a strong political will here to keep a major public service on...there is a patriarchal belief...that the public sector actually does things very well for a local community.' A number of interviewees referred simply to the feeling of 'pride in municipal services' and one Director, in an authority with no overall control, expressed the view of many when he referred to local authority members who

> do not like to lose large parts of the organization that they've put a lot of time and effort into, they've got emotionally involved in – and particularly in large buildings. Members look and say, 'Look, that's the end product of the amount of time I've spent on that Council.'

Thus there was no straightforward relationship between party political control and support for the retention of a significant local authority service-providing role. That is not to suggest, however, that there were no discernible variations in attitudes to the encouragement of private sector provision. This issue is addressed further in the following section.

Doubts about alternative provision

The reservations expressed about non-statutory sector provision concerned, on the one hand, what local authorities perceived to be the variable willingness and ability of alternative providers to develop service-providing roles as well as local authorities' own reluctance to encourage some of these providers. In the latter case, this reluctance was expressed in a preference for voluntary and not-for-profit agencies. Just as there was no straightforward relationship between councils' political control and their support for retaining a service-providing role, so was there no straightforward relationship between political control and encouragement or discouragement of the private sector.

Nevertheless, while no Conservative-controlled authority said it would actively discourage private providers, considerable doubts about the private sector were expressed in four Labour-controlled authorities. Indeed, two of them said that the private sector would not be considered at all, the Chair of one approvingly quoting a colleague's view 'that as a last resort we'd sooner burn the [local authority] homes as let them go private'. Less extreme were the views in the other two authorities: that 'unless the [private] organizations are set up with a more altruistic view than they have had in the past I can't see them delivering the type of service we want'; and that there is 'a very strong suspicion of the profit motive in health and community care'.

It was further evident that many authorities had serious doubts about the potential of both for-profit and not-for-profit agencies to increase significantly their contribution to a mixed economy. In terms of the private sector's contribution, three main concerns were expressed:

- the types of client to be cared for;
- the effects of funding patterns and changes; and
- the extent of authorities' knowledge and awareness of private sector potential.

The view made explicitly by only two Directors, but alluded to by a number of others, was that private sector agencies provide for only the least dependent individuals. According to one of these Directors, 'It's a very important point that the private sector isn't providing for people with high dependency or special needs...private residential homes won't look after someone of very severe dementia or physical disability.' He accepted that there was more potential in respect of non-acute care, but 'as soon as you begin to get into high dependency...the organizations you've got here are not best suited: they haven't got the skills, the professionalism, the expertise'. This general argument was contested by some private sector representatives, who argued that private agencies would indeed be prepared to operate services for such individuals. In evidence to the House of Commons Health Committee in 1993, the United Kingdom Home Care Association asserted categorically that 'contrary to some people's beliefs, the independent sector does cater for heavily dependent people' (UKHCA 1993: 2). Accepting that such services would be expensive, it was suggested during our study that they could nevertheless be made a commercially viable proposition if bought, for example, by a consortium of neighbouring local authorities.

The second concern about funding patterns and changes, voiced in a small number of authorities, was that unless income support levels were raised sufficiently, the squeeze on residential care home proprietors would drive some out of business before 1993. Some local authorities anticipated that to counteract this possibility there would be an accelerating shift to nursing home provision, and a smaller number anticipated that private agencies would diversify into day care or domiciliary care. It has to be said, however, that such expectations were in most cases entirely speculative, and based on little or no discussion with existing local private providers, who had rarely been included in service planning and design (see also Chapter 6). It was evident that some authorities had acknowledged and begun to address this problem and sought to create coordinating mechanisms which included private providers. However, these were a minority. The Department of Health's own concern about this situation led it to commission KPMG, in January 1992, to investigate the extent of independent sector involvement in planning processes. The results of this study (referred to elsewhere) bore out our own finding about the general lack of private sector involvement in particular (KPMG 1992). More fundamentally, we also found a basic ignorance of this sector. It is interesting, for example, to note the view of the Chair in one Labour-controlled council that:

> At the member level we have been fairly neutral on this...we ourselves don't have links with the private sector...for most of us...the private sector is an unknown quantity. I don't use it personally; I don't know constituents who do; I don't get complaints about it. So it's all a bit of a mystery trying to access it. And clearly it wouldn't be top of my list of priorities of things to do.

At the same time, there was a broad consensus about the great uncertainty among voluntary organizations about the merits of developing as service providers. This uncertainty was either because the organizations perceived themselves to be ill-equipped – in management terms – to shift to a tighter contractual relationship with local authority or health authority purchasers, or because such a move was seen as potentially undermining or compromising their traditional lobbying, campaigning and advocacy roles. While it was clear that many voluntary organizations had not concluded this internal debate, it was also clear that some local authorities were taking a more active part than others in aiding the debate by initiating discussion of the implications.

Moreover, it was a widely held view across our sample that the majority of the voluntary organizations in any locality were ill-equipped to become significant service providers. One Director contended that because of their 'smallness and volunteer base' the voluntary organizations in his area were 'very frightened by the contract culture and felt they were in no position to start drawing up tenders, etc.' Another Director, in a county council, argued that 'the level of skill...the level of maturity of those organizations – their capacity to look beyond the next six months – is low'; as a result, he said 'the indigenous voluntary sector is going to be a slow growth area'. And in another county council, the Director likewise maintained that 'most voluntary organizations are in no position to take on a significant role in contracting. It could totally change the nature of their organization; they haven't got the organizational status.'

In each of these cases, local authority perceptions of voluntary sector potential were couched in terms of ability rather than willingness of voluntary organizations to become more significant providers. In many authorities there was thought to be a genuine willingness, among *some* local voluntary organizations, but still either limited ability or managerial underdevelopment. The Chair of one authority with long experience of working with voluntary organizations said that although there was 'in many cases a willingness...there equally is considerable alarm at the prospect of what it is they might be going to be asked to do...many of these organizations at the moment are organized on a shoestring in terms of resources and management and back up.'

There are, however, two general points to be made about this local authority perception of the voluntary sector potential to help create, and operate within, a larger mixed economy. First, it was not a unanimous view: in three authorities, officers and members claimed that there were well developed networks of local voluntary organizations capable of contributing significantly within an enlarged mixed economy. Moreover, it was said, they were well developed precisely because of a history of local authority support – financial and managerial – and encouragement. Second, in discounting the potential contribution of 'the voluntary sector', most authorities made an exception for the 'brand-name' organizations which nationally have developed an expertise as large service providing agencies – for example, Mind, Mencap and Age Concern. However, the local branches of these large national agencies not only retain considerable or complete autonomy, but also have extremely variable capacities. In many localities, even local branches of these large national organizations may either be undecided about their future role or be insufficiently developed to embrace the contract culture. As one social services Director said of a local Mencap group, it was composed almost entirely of parents and carers who, quite understandably, had neither the time nor the energy to devote to running what was, in effect, a business.

This leads us finally, and briefly, to one other crucial area in which the non-statutory sector potential for partnership in increased service provision was held to be limited: the potential of the informal sector. Many Directors and Chairs, as well as interviewees in other agencies, argued that it was vital to recognize the crucial role already played by informal carers as *the* main providers of community care. It was said to be equally vital not to overestimate how much more they could be expected to do. Thus, as the Chair in one authority argued, carers 'are pretty heavily burdened already with actually keeping granny going, or whatever'. A fellow Chair was equally pessimistic:

> I'm not sure the informal care sector is able to take on much more: in fact, we see the trend going the other way, that people are beginning to resist these very large commitments...with the trend of women going back to work, I think we may come to real difficulties.

Detailed organizational reactions

Our fieldwork also covered the organizational responses which authorities were making to the proposals set out in the legislation and subsequent policy guidance. These responses fell into three main categories: organizational arrangements within social services departments; corporate responsibilities; and external relationships. We summarize our principal findings for each of these categories.

Internal arrangements

Ten of the twenty-four sample authorities created some form of development budget or dedicated resource to facilitate implementation, the majority of which (six) were county councils. Of the latter, sums ranged from £60,000 to appoint new research staff, to £250,000 and £350,000 to establish separate community care implementation units or teams responsible for coordinating the work of planning groups and for such specific tasks as compiling resource inventories.

Nine authorities employed external consultants to advise on preparations for implementation. Three authorities used single individuals, two of whom gave advice and made recommendations on the options for residential home transfers (see Chapter 7). Four other authorities employed management consultants for this same purpose, but only two authorities engaged such firms to advise on management arrangements themselves.

In nine authorities, primary responsibility for implementation was that of single lead officers in the social services departments, three of whom were newly appointed to these posts. Four of these lead officers were part of separately created units to manage the implementation of the changes. In the other cases they were typically responsible for the coordination of newly formed project or planning groups. One authority had established working parties to shadow the Social Services Inspectorate's groups and two others were part of a regional network of authorities with similar shadow groups. Elsewhere there was a considerable diversity in the range of project groups established. One Director referred to having established project groups 'for everything that moves...you name it, we've got it', whereas another authority had established just two project groups – one for assessment and one for purchasing.

Corporate responsibility

In the majority of authorities (seventeen), implementation of the NHS and Community Care Act was said to be clearly a corporate responsibility, although what this meant in practice varied considerably. In only one authority was there evidence of the sort of overarching strategy for service development implied by *Caring for People*:

Social care and practical assistance with daily living are key components of good quality community care. The services and facilities, at present largely the responsibility of social services authorities, which will be essential to enable people to live in the community include help with personal and domestic tasks such as cleaning, washing and preparing meals, with disablement equipment and home adaptations, transport, budgeting and other aspects of daily living. Suitable good quality housing is essential and the availability of day care, respite care, leisure facilities and employment and educational opportunities will all improve the quality of life enjoyed by a person with care needs. (Secretaries of State 1989b: para. 2.4)

In two authorities, community care was described as an 'agreed corporate priority' and as 'a corporate priority although the management of it and the implementation of it was being handled by the SSD'. In each of them, however, community care was a corporate issue in the sense of being a priority for resource allocation rather than for corporate policy or service development. Other authorities expressed the corporate dimension only in general terms; as, for example, 'very much part of the (authority's) corporate approach' or something which the authority 'looked at in the broadest possible way'. In others it was no more than a 'corporate agenda issue' about which the Director kept fellow chief officers informed. In one authority, however, it was a corporate responsibility in the sense of the community care plan being a personal objective of the chief executive.

One particular issue which was, however, seen to be a much more concrete corporate responsibility was the transfer of residential homes. In each of the authorities concerned (see Chapter 7), this was regarded 'as a really important corporate matter' which needed not just to have a broader member perspective but also to draw upon expertise from the chief executive's, secretary's, and land and property departments.

This specific issue apart, the adoption of a corporate view usually involved the establishment of a range of officer (rather than member) forums. Six authorities referred to having member coordinating groups generally matching similar officer groups, and in two authorities these were said to be all-party groups. In other authorities there were no such formal mechanisms but, instead, the customary use of controlling-party groups, or the regular informal meetings of leading Chairs, or the overlapping membership of the relevant service committees (such as housing and education). Another means of seeking to ensure a corporate commitment referred to by a number of authorities was the holding of member seminars. However, some Chairs spoke of their difficulty in interesting other council members. For example, one Chair of a Labour-controlled council said that 'community care actually hasn't got the level of member involvement or member interest as some other areas do... everyone gets excited by education matters'. Similarly, the Conservative group leader of a hung council said that despite organizing 'consciousness-raising conferences' for members 'I think I could speak of some members of the committees who don't even know about it'. The relative ignorance or lack of interest in community care was contrasted with the far greater level and breadth of member interest in the Children Act, attributed to the greater visibility and immediacy of issues such as child abuse.

External arrangements

Coordinating machinery for other statutory and non-statutory agencies
In view of the long-standing and well-established criticisms of the formal joint planning machinery – Joint Consultative Committees and Joint Care Planning Teams (see, for example, Wistow 1988, 1990b; Hardy *et al.* 1989) – one striking aspect of the responses across the twenty-four authorities was the number in which it was said that this existing formal machinery was being used successfully as the forum for community care planning. Among the seven London boroughs, for example, one referred to the positive work of the existing joint planning arrangements in preparing for implementation of the community care changes. All had coterminous boundaries with the health service.

By contrast, in only one county council – none of which in the sample had the advantage of one-to-one coterminosity – was the current formal joint machinery said to be an adequate basis for the effective coordination of community care planning. In most of the other county councils working relationships with health authorities were described as good, with new coordinating mechanisms having been established (augmenting the existing structures) either at the level of informal but regular chief officer meetings or in client group teams. Three county councils were in the process of revising their joint planning machinery; one because 'none of (the Joint Consultative Committee/ Joint Care Planning Team machinery) is necessary any more' and another in response to major structural change involving amalgamations among its health authorities.

The position in the seven metropolitan districts was a more mixed one: in none was there any reference to having the sort of effective formal joint arrangements mentioned in the London boroughs. As with the sample as a whole, most of the authorities had established community care steering/project groups (which usually included health representatives) and client-group or topic-related working groups.

Seven authorities referred to their growing problems in adjusting to or synchronizing with health authority agendas and timetables. One county council Director referred to health authorities being driven into 'short-term survival deals'. Another Director referred to the 'quite alarming' changes in the health service. 'We haven't been part of their planning process at the beginning: we are involved three-quarters along the way and that makes things difficult...we've certainly been left behind; we haven't gone together in planning.' In terms of the involvement of other statutory agencies, there was said to be limited involvement of education departments across all authorities and there was difficulty for some counties (four out of ten) in collaborating with their district councils: 'we're not in very close touch with [them], they're very many and very diverse'; and 'trying to get them to talk to each other is bad enough, let alone talk to us'. In the remaining authorities (county councils as well as metropolitan districts and London boroughs) there were often said to be close links with housing authorities and departments. One explanation for the limited involvement of other agencies was that the major changes for social services departments (and the health service) were occurring simultaneously with comparably significant changes in both education and housing departments. Engaging either department in community care changes was inevitably difficult, it was argued, when many were being virtually overwhelmed by their own changes and associated problems.

Our main finding about the involvement of non-statutory agencies was that, whereas voluntary sector agencies were generally well-represented within coordinating mechanisms, private sector agencies were generally excluded. In most authorities, arrangements to increase voluntary sector representation were said to be mere developments of what already existed, albeit at a pace accelerated by the White Paper and Act. However, two authorities had initiated the formation of voluntary sector forums as a result of the legislation (one of which also appointed a coordinator for three years, from joint finance), and two others had held one-day conferences to inform voluntary organizations of proposed changes.

As indicated earlier, comparable arrangements to involve private sector providers did not exist. Only two of the twenty-four authorities said that the private sector was involved in current planning groups. In four other authorities, there was said to be 'an increasing dialogue', 'a series of meetings', 'regular meetings with proprietors of nursing homes' and 'a series of discussions'. In one other authority, a day conference was planned replicating that held for voluntary organizations. Other than these arrangements, private sector involvement was limited. In one authority this limited involvement was said to be because 'we're struggling to be clear what to say to them at this time'. But in two other authorities the non-involvement amounted to deliberate exclusion: according to one Director, 'not quite deliberate but practically deliberate', and in the other authority they were 'just not involved; they weren't invited and they were kept at more than arm's length'. In this latter case, however, it was added that the 'barriers have begun to break down'.

In mitigation, it was said that the main problem for local authorities positively seeking to involve private sector agencies was that typically the latter were poorly represented on their own coordinating forums (where those existed) and frequently consisted of small-scale organizations without the time to devote to time-consuming joint planning forums. This problem was acknowledged by one private sector representative who admitted that locally there had been 'no coordinated response whatsoever'. His local association had always had a minority of members, and had never generated a relationship which has been able to give us a coordinated attitude and response to any change. We've always tended to pull our own little ways, look upon our own businesses in isolation unfortunately. And we can do no more than blame ourselves on that one, but that is the situation.

Mechanisms to involve users and carers

One of the main thrusts of the legislative changes was to increase the involvement of users and carers in the process of care planning, design and delivery, and the importance of this facet of the changes has been often underlined by Health Ministers (see, for example, Mawhinney 1992). Three general points emerged in our study. First, there was universal support for the principle of involving users and carers in service planning and delivery, although the tangible steps taken to involve them varied considerably. Second, the legislation had given an additional and more specific impetus to develop appropriate mechanisms, however widespread the general commitment to the principle was beforehand. Third, authorities generally acknowledged the need to be proactive in encouraging and supporting user and carer involvement. The *Caring For People* White Paper's assertion that 'the great bulk of community care is provided by friends, family and neighbours' (Secretaries of State 1989b: para. 1.9), was unquestioned, as was the importance of the government's objective of ensuring 'that service providers make practical support for carers a high priority' (*ibid.*: para. 1.11). As with community care itself, involvement of and support for carers was taken to be a self-evident 'good', although as one of our national respondents remarked in respect of carers' current 'visibility', the scope of the attitudinal change that this represents in the past ten years is enormous.

There was much less consensus about precisely how carers and users can be involved in service planning and delivery – other than at the stage of individual assessment, which was generally taken to be, at least in principle, relatively straightforward. In terms of arrangements pre-dating the legislation, two of the authorities had a dedicated carer support budget and staff, and two others had established carers' forums or councils. Some other authorities also supported, financially and otherwise, local branches of the Carers National Association and many more referred to their support (typically through joint finance) for Crossroads Care schemes. Even where such support schemes existed, however, some doubts were expressed about their success in increasing significantly carers' involvement.

A commonly voiced concern was the difficulty of 'getting in touch properly' with the majority of service users and carers. For example, one Director referred to the tendency for voluntary organizations 'to represent carers more than users', and one Chair referred to the 'fairly familiar...trap of listening to the most vocal people within the community'. The problem, he said, was that of:

professional users or professional carers, people who know the local authority and the system and the way it works and tap in to the bureaucratic structures...and the local authority have been encouraging that in only listening to those kind of users and carers who can tap into its own structure.

The general conclusion across the twenty-four sample authorities, borne out in a subsequent analysis of the first round of community care plans (Wistow et al. 1993) was that mechanisms to involve carers and users in service design and delivery were in most cases at no more than an embryonic stage of development. Against that background there was a consensus not only about the difficulty of ensuring such involvement, but also about the financial costs of seeking to do so. In some authorities users and carers will continue to participate in client group planning teams, but in most they are yet to be represented on such teams.

Summary

There were some clearly discernible similarities in authorities' reactions to the change agenda created by the legislation and guidance. First, there was widespread support for the service philosophy and principles: support in the case of many authorities because these principles accorded with the direction in which the authorities were already travelling. Second, except for the local authority lead role, there was a widespread scepticism about the organizational principles underlying the changes, that is the enabling role (seen as market development) and the creation of a mixed economy of – and especially a market in – social care. Third, there was near universal uncertainty and anxiety about resources.

These inherent local authority reservations were increased by a series of related factors. First, authorities had other priorities in terms of both the implementation of the Children Act and the introduction – as part of the community care changes – of, for example, inspection units and complaints procedures. Second, local authorities had, on the one hand, a considerable pride in their own previous service provision and, on the other, serious doubts about the potential of alternative providing agendas to develop a service-providing role. Finally, the government's decision to delay the implementation timetable fuelled fears among local authorities about its long-term commitment to the changes: a commitment, nevertheless, repeatedly emphasized by successive government ministers, (for example, Mawhinney 1992; and the two Foster/Laming letters: Department of Health 1992b, c). At the time of our study, however, these fears – allied to other priorities, resource anxieties and uncertainties following the general election – led to the generally cautious response among local authorities.

This mood of caution and reluctance was borne out by the relatively modest scale and pace of direct investment in authorities' own mechanisms for implementing the changes. There were, however, some notable exceptions.

A few authorities – including some of those least enthusiastic about the changes – had created significant budgets for implementation machinery and in some areas – notably residential home transfers – there was more activity than passivity. Even here, however, as we discuss in Chapter 7, authorities' principal motivation in such transfers was to take advantage of perceived financial incentives rather than a commitment to develop a mixed economy of care.

5

Building a mixed economy

Introduction

Moving England's social care system towards the White Paper vision of a mixed economy requires the careful nurturing of new modes of provision and the gradual introduction of new commissioning routes. The White Paper readily acknowledged that it would take a long time to bring about the proposed supply and funding reforms in their entirety, even assuming the political and professional will in local authorities. In contrast to the requirements placed on health authorities to separate the purchasing and providing roles immediately and introduce an internal market, albeit while maintaining a 'steady state' in the first year, social services departments were urged to 'introduce changes at a pace appropriate to their organisation' (Department of Health 1990a: 1). Such guidance suggests that the Department of Health envisaged that the full development of a mixed economy would take place over several years rather than months. At the same time, however, as we argued in Chapter 2, social services departments would have to manage an external market of independent sector providers from April 1993. As will become clear, the nature of this implementation task was not fully appreciated. Indeed, even the concept of a social care market was either resisted or well to the back of authorities' consciousness.

The delayed implementation gave further reason for circumspection in the process of change. By early 1991, a number of authorities had reached only the early stages of a mixed economy. Some were also hoping that the election of a Labour government would mean not having to proceed to any later developmental stages. In this chapter we consider how local authorities viewed the prospect of developing a mixed economy of care, and what actions they were initiating.

As we described in Chapter 3, a mixed economy has two principal dimensions – alternative modes of provision and sources of funding – which together define various broad arrangements for the delivery and purchase of services. Enthusiastically or otherwise, local authorities are currently following the broad government line in emphasizing the development of a mixed economy of provision, with little active planning of a mixed economy of funding. They certainly had new funding *responsibilities* from April 1993, but were generally not yet actively encouraging the injection of finances from sources other than themselves or the health authority. Indeed, the social security transfer represented a one-off diminution in the variety of funding sources. In describing attitudes and actions concerning the funding of community care, our account must therefore inevitably concentrate more on mechanisms than sources.

Reduced to its basic elements, the NHS and Community Care Act legislates for changes in three areas of the mixed economy.

- The first is the baseline from which local authorities and other bodies should build community care services, the Act requiring the mapping of need and supply, and the publication of annual community care plans which bring the two together.
- Second, authorities should consider changes to their organizational structures and incentives so as to encourage better planning and delivery, the separation of purchasers from providers being a key recommendation.
- Third, the Act seeks to encourage a larger number and broader range of providers, with local authorities being asked specifically to facilitate the development of non-statutory providers.

How were authorities tackling these three tasks up to spring 1991?

Mapping needs

The major challenge of the new social care system for purchasers, whether whole authorities seeking to plan their expenditures or individual care managers establishing frameworks for responding to their assessments of clients' circumstances, is to map needs and demands. Needs are usually taken to mean felt, expressed or adjudged shortfalls in individual welfare, whereas demands are those expressed shortfalls which are backed by the power to secure the means to meet them. A free market in social care, without any welfare state safety net, would see services allocated solely on the basis of purchasing power: those who can pay will get services. The early post-war vision of welfare services saw allocations determined solely by need: services were to be free at the point of delivery, save for some nominal charges. The reality of the past four decades has obviously been somewhere between these two polar extremes, with public authorities struggling to identify needs and then find the resources to meet them, and therefore sometimes charging users to raise revenues, while wealthier individuals and families have remained free to purchase services from independent providers. The plans for community care in the 1990s do not, in themselves, represent a departure from the dominant post-war experience. In fact, insofar as the 1989 White Paper placed more emphasis on *needs*-based planning than any other post-war government policy document, it is arguable that the principle has been given considerable reinforcement.

Some local authorities have long maintained that there is no point in mapping needs if the resources are not there to meet them (Audit Commission 1992a: para. 34). Most authorities continue to fear that they will not have the resources to meet the needs which they identify, and that – *de facto*, if not *de jure* – the reality of the 1990s will be demand-based allocation.

How, then, were local authorities identifying or mapping needs? 'Dreadfully; we are struggling' was one Director's terse response, and he went on to describe the new management information system that had been purchased, 'although the prospect of ever getting it up and running is pretty remote because of our financial position'. Another Director described the task as 'a headache', illustrating the difficulties by listing his department's trawl for information from current service users, referrals, people on waiting lists, consultation meetings with population groups to gain their perceptions about needs, and annual public health reports. In a third authority a similar jigsaw was being assembled, and the Director's description of their current activities was fairly typical:

> We are starting with population figures, known clients and all the information systems, and putting it together to try to work out the bottom line figure. What we *are* doing now is clearly exchanging information with health authorities in a more explicit way than we have done before – with family health services authorities and key voluntary organizations as well. I don't think that is going to get us much beyond 85 per cent of the realistic position, but it will be a much better position than we have been in before.

In at least seven of our twenty-four sample areas, local and health authorities were planning joint strategies for gathering information.

The irrelevance of waiting lists was recognized: people might be 'on a waiting list for a day centre because we cannot get them home care or some other service that they would prefer'. In another area, the authority 'is overwhelmed with demand...We have got 1,000 people on waiting lists for day care for under fives; the need is probably about 200 or 300 places.' Social services or education department registers of people with learning disabilities were often reported as being fairly accurate, and more than one Director commented that the needs and preferences of people with physical disabilities were made known to them on a regular basis, but the general picture was not good. Identifying the needs of elderly people and people with mental health problems posed greater difficulties, and the application of national estimates of prevalence rates to projected local demographic trends was usually the most sophisticated top-down needs measurement that authorities could expect to have available for some time.

Only a few authorities reported using delegated responsibilities to care managers to measure needs alongside top-down, statistical exercises to gain authority-wide and longer-term perspectives. One authority had set up a network of community mental health teams with responsibility

> to map the territory and to stimulate provision and develop services which met the needs of their community. That was real bottom-up planning. The only bit we were doing at the centre was appointing them and bringing them back periodically to say: What have you found so far? Then we aggregated. The county plan was a real aggregation of what they had found. The only way we could map the territory was to put some people down there to actually find out what was needed.

Overall, by early 1991, six authorities reported that they were actively mapping needs already, but a similar number had made no progress in deciding how they were going to identify or measure need (Table 5.1). When we looked more carefully at this pattern of responses, we found no relationship between action in the mapping of needs and either political control or authority type, and no consistent or particularly strong links with levels of spending or support for the non-statutory sectors.

It is clear from a subsequent analysis of the 1992 community care plans that the comprehensive mapping of needs remains one of the major challenges facing local authorities (Wistow *et al.* 1993). The comparatively high cost of obtaining information on needs provides one of the largest potential obstacles to the smooth functioning of social care markets (see Chapter 6). Moreover, since our study was completed, the political costs associated with the mapping

Table 5.1 Attitudes and actions concerning the development of a mixed economy of care as of early 1991

Component/element in building a mixed economy	Number of authorities with	
	Positive attitude	Action
Mapping needs	18	6
Purchaser/provider split	7	1
Budgetary devolution	11	2
Residential home trusts	16	6
Management buy-outs etc.	7	0
Service specifications, contracts	18	12
Joint purchasing	9	6
Market encouragement	6	6
Total number of authorities	24	24

of need have become more apparent (Wistow and Hardy 1993). The Department of Health has indicated that it will not be collecting and collating information about unmet need. This, according to one of the government's own backbenchers, 'negates the whole principle that community care should be driven by needs rather than resources' (House of Commons Health Committee 1993b). Guidance from the Department of Health on this issue has left at least some authorities concerned that they may be open to legal challenge (Wistow and Hardy 1993) if they record unmet needs. Describing such guidance as 'unhelpful', the Health Select Committee recommended 'that clear guidance be issued urgently...and, if necessary, legislation introduced to make sure that there are no inhibitions on the ability of social services departments and health authorities to make a full assessment of unmet needs' (House of Commons Health Committee 1993a).

The purchaser/provider split

The government has urged local authorities to consider changes in their organizational structures. A needs-led approach, it has argued, 'presupposes a progressive separation of assessment from service provision' (Department of Health 1990a: 25). One of the 1990 Act's most fundamental contributions to a mixed economy could be the flexibility and power it gives to care managers. Under the right conditions, the most important influences of market forces could come at a case level, affording greater choice for care managers and clients. The autonomy to be enjoyed will largely be determined by the extent and dimensions of the split between purchaser and provider functions. The split has at least four elements (compare Department of Health 1991b).

- The *starting point*: the point at the top of an authority or social services department (SSD) at which the split begins. In the extreme, the Director might be the only employee not allocated to one of the purchasing or providing arms.
- The *end point*: the lowest level in the department to which the split extends. At the other extreme, there might be individual assessing and purchasing care managers, who provide no services themselves, working alongside providers who do no assessing.
- The *financial empowerment*: the extent of budgetary devolution and the services covered. Opposite extremes would be the Director in one authority who told us how he bought his desk in two halves to keep within his limited discretionary budget, and, in another authority, the care managers with client-specific budgets who are allowed to purchase residential care placements.
- The *component responsibilities*: the range of activities which are allocated to the purchaser and provider arms, such as training, personnel, financial management or advice, legal advice and so on.

By early 1991, few authorities had drawn up precise plans for the purchaser/
provider split (Table 5.1). Only two had already achieved some degree of
split, and another had been conducting a small pilot project. Of the others,
one had no intention of such a reorganization, and seven were not intending
to introduce such a split unless forced. (Two were hoping for a Labour
government before April 1993, but councils controlled by each of the main
political parties were among the reluctant. Most saw the split as inevitable,
but, faced with so many other pressures, welcomed the delay.) The other
sample authorities expressed intentions which ranged from a cautious 'possibly
but slowly', to a definite commitment to a split whose details had yet to be
agreed. None of these authorities reported using the opportunity of phased
implementation to conduct (new) pilot trials, and few had decided how the
purchaser/provider split would affect their committee structures. Directors of
social services were almost universally more enthusiastic than members about
splitting the purchasing and providing functions, and some reported that
members did not yet understand this aspect of the community care reforms.

This slow progress in formulating plans for a purchaser/provider split
was understandable insofar as the new arrangements did not need to be in
place before 1993, and because of the complexity of any such reorganization
(Department of Health 1991b; Lawson 1991; Means 1991). Political and
professional factors also exerted some influence. Some authorities adhered to
the ideological premise that 'no local authority should run anything commercial', and some politicians simply sought to protect the authority's own
provision, fearing that the purchaser/provider split would remove services
from their control. At least two authorities (one Labour and one Conservative)
saw no logic in splitting their SSDs until a mixed economy of supply existed,
and the difficulties of achieving competition among providers in rural areas
prompted reservations in some of the shires. A small number of interviewees
saw the administrative simplicity and ease of financial control associated with
block contracts as more attractive than the need to offer care managers and
clients a range of options by devolving decision-making powers and budgets.
As this finding demonstrates, therefore, it is not inevitable that a split between
purchasers and providers will enhance user choice. Recognizing the reluctance
of authorities to introduce the split, the Audit Commission (1992a: para. 72)
has recommended that they alter the balance away from central towards local
commissioning through care management by gradually adjusting the funds
devolved to the local level as confidence grows and information systems are
improved.

Support for a split between the purchasing and providing functions came
from a number of quarters. One interviewee argued that the split was essential
to identify the true costs of public sector provision and to ensure no favouritism
in the market for contracts, although another reluctantly accepted the need
for a split as an *alternative* to contracting-out. There were, in fact, a number
of reasons for making the split (Knapp and Wistow 1993). First, it provides
an opportunity to strengthen functions which otherwise tend to be sub-

ordinated to the day-to-day demands of operational management, including needs analysis, specification of desired outcomes, accurate identification of the costs of decisions, ensuring a match between needs and resources, and evaluation and review. A second reason for separating purchasing and providing is to weaken the influence of provider vested interests in service specification and hence to strengthen the possibility that service design will reflect user rather than provider needs. It also facilitates collaboration between social services departments and the NHS, where the purchaser/provider split is now a well-established fact of organizational life.

Reactions to government recommendations to *devolve budgetary powers* are summarized in Table 5.1. Local authorities' actions and attitudes concerning budgetary devolution were strongly correlated with their actions and attitudes concerning a purchaser/provider split. Where budgetary devolution or a purchaser/provider split was seen as the precursor for some form of internal market, authorities were generally cautious about moving forward; where it was seen as a natural prerequisite for greater client choice it was often embraced with enthusiasm. There was, however, widespread concern that current financial management and information systems were simply inadequate to support delegated decision-making. Some Directors had long been frustrated by their finance departments' policies on budgetary devolution. As one commented,

> They can agree a social worker can take a child into care, but they won't agree to them spending five pence...The only thing here which perhaps would help is that our Director of Finance retires soon; we are looking forward to more flexibility from that point onwards.

Another SSD had only recently wrested control of training and financial management from central departments, and in at least two authorities decisions on grants to voluntary organizations were taken by central committees without necessarily canvassing the views of the social services committee. In these cases, social care policies and priorities were not the primary reason for grant-funding even when the organizations were providing social care services.

Care manager budgets were far from popular. 'Kent went too far' was the view of one Director (from outside Kent!), in reference to that county's pioneering efforts with devolved budgets. Another Director was worried about 'field social workers running around with cheque books'. On the other hand, there was support from a number of people for the argument that 'the expectations of the customer and the ability to pay have to be linked together'.

Joint purchasing

In the long term, England's social care system may need more mixing of the economy of *funding*, although in 1991 local authorities' plans in this direction were confined to considerations of joint purchasing. Four local authorities had taken the decision *not* to pursue joint purchasing. Only one authority was already engaged in a number of joint purchasing schemes with health authorities, although pilot or demonstration projects were found in five other areas. These pilots were for people with learning disabilities (mental handicaps), mental health problems or HIV/AIDS, and in most but not all cases had been sufficiently successful to encourage some replication. One authority was hoping to introduce care management for mental health services, if joint purchasing arrangements could be agreed with the district health authority, and would treat this as a pilot for other services. The health authority concerned was less confident about the speed with which these arrangements could be introduced. Generally, local authorities were undecided (ten cases), and usually had not discussed it at all, or had agreed with their local health authorities (districts and regions, and sometimes also family health services authorities) that joint purchasing would be introduced once they had recovered from other organizational changes (three cases). From our observations and a preliminary analysis of available statistical data, we would hypothesize that joint purchasing is more likely to be found in local authorities with lower per capita spending and higher levels of contracting-out of services.

Reservations about joint purchasing included concerns about the quality of communication between the two statutory bodies, and the common observation that health authorities had too many other things to deal with at the moment. Local authorities, for their part, were giving greater priority to the introduction of new assessment procedures and a purchaser/provider split. This disjunction between local and health authority agendas and timetables was perceived to be an obstacle to closer working in seven authorities. There was no evidence that the problem was either more prevalent or more acute where health service units had been granted trust status, although one Director referred to 'uncertainty over the trusts, which has been a major problem'. Another Director referred to his authority's main priority as 'trying to keep abreast of health authority developments, whilst not being able to move into our own configurations because of resource constraints'. Differences in priorities caused more difficulties when counties had to liaise with two or more health authorities. As the Director of one of these counties remarked,

> The health authorities are driven into short-term survival deals. Therefore when we say 'Can we talk about the wider implications of all this and what's going to happen after 1993?', the answer is: 'I have got to get these people out of the hospital by Friday'. When everybody is in that kind of short-term survival mode it doesn't really facilitate anything other than gross opportunism: that's the danger.

A fellow Director argued that it was not just the different pace of change that was the problem but the 'less than 100 per cent commitment by the health authorities' to develop a mixed economy of care in partnership with the local authority and other agencies. It is, he said, 'all going to come down to the fact that we're all going to be protective of our own resources'. A problem for some authorities was that districts were considering merging, but doing so outside any joint health authority/local authority framework.

The policy guidance makes it clear how vital the Department of Health regards joint working between local and health authorities (1990a: paras 1.7–1.11). It is noteworthy how many sample authorities reported the development of good joint mechanisms with health authorities (see Chapter 4), in many cases building on well-developed formal Joint Consultative Committee/Joint Care Planning Team machinery. Since 1991, joint commissioning has been more widely discussed by local and health authorities, with numerous potential advantages as well as difficulties (Knapp *et al.* 1992b).

Encouraging a mixed economy of supply

One of the six key objectives of the community care White Paper is 'to promote the development of a flourishing independent sector alongside good quality public services' (Secretaries of State 1989b: para. 1.11). Strong encouragement has been given to pluralism and diversification in community care provision, more recently reflected in the central government directive that 85 per cent of the money transferred from the social security budget be spent on services in the independent sector.

There was considerable local authority interest in establishing semi- or fully independent trusts to run residential care facilities in order to shift a substantial financial burden on to social security budgets (see Chapter 7), and some authorities explored the options of management buy-outs and employee share ownership schemes. However, in early 1991, no authority reported having a comprehensive view of current provision, although some were confident that recent efforts to establish information systems would eventually get them closer. Services which were required to register (such as residential care facilities), or which received financial or other tangible support from the authority, or whose establishment had been preceded by a planning or change-of-use application, were obviously known, and their capabilities and limitations usually well appreciated. Local voluntary sector umbrella groups often compiled directories of services with the financial support of the local authority. But private and some voluntary day and domiciliary services were less well known, while informal, neighbourhood and self-care activities were rarely mentioned when we asked interviewees about supply. With few immediate intentions or incentives to fund, or in other ways support, non-statutory non-residential services, and with numerous more pressing uses for scarce administrative resources, the mapping of supply was clearly often a low priority.

There were exceptions, of course. It was mentioned on more than one occasion that bottom-up mapping was a necessary early task of a decentralized purchasing system. Authorities planning to devolve decision-making and perhaps budgetary responsibilities had generally recognized the needs for improving supply information. Authorities fortunate enough to be coterminous with health authorities had the opportunity to conduct joint audits or mappings, although these were rare in practice. A subsequent analysis of a sample of the first-round community care plans (which had been published in April 1992) confirmed these findings; only a minority of authorities had gone beyond the production of limited service inventories and attempted a more systematic mapping of resources (Wistow *et al.* 1993).

However, with other facets of the community care reforms pressing and, in 1991, with no immediate financial or other incentives to encourage pluralism in domiciliary, day or respite care, authorities had gathered little formal or reliable information on the full range of social care services in their areas. Non-statutory residential and nursing homes were rather different. Local authorities necessarily had a fairly good view of the former through their registration and inspection activities. They also had strong incentives to acquire more information about both residential and nursing home provision because they were to assume responsibility for funding non-statutory placements after April 1993.

Trusts

One of the most important forces behind the move towards a mixed economy is the promotion of efficiency and effectiveness. Experience has led authorities to be cautious of the dangers of pursuing economy rather than efficiency and effectiveness. As they considered the development of a mixed economy, they were sensitive, therefore, to the need to protect traditional service principles while taking whichever financial advantages were available. The transfer of residential homes to the private and voluntary sectors was the principal area in which such gains were identified, but was dependent upon transferring the care costs to the social security system: an option which would be foreclosed when the community care changes were fully implemented in 1993.

In this context the most attractive option to many authorities was to establish organizations which were sufficiently independent for their clients to be eligible for DSS funding, but nevertheless sufficiently linked for the authority to retain some control over staffing, admissions or quality of care. In this book, we refer to these new organizations as *trusts*, although a variety of legal forms was established. Each of the trusts in our sample of authorities was built around an existing organization, usually a housing association. Six authorities had already set up a not-for-profit trust or some other statutory–voluntary hybrid, and a further three had made a decision in principle to do so. A further seven authorities seemed likely to establish such arrangements but were taking legal advice because of doubts about their legality and whether residents would attract social security benefits.

Five authorities considered trusts and ruled them out. Two (one Conservative and one no overall control) preferred to sell local authority services to the private sector; one Labour council had ruled out any movement of services from the authority; and two Conservative authorities were similarly intent to retain their own services, one of them having faced political difficulties in recent years after disposing of other local authority services. Authorities which had taken or were taking steps to set up residential home trusts tended not to have made much progress with service specifications, although they did not express negative attitudes to such specifications. This is a clear indication that there is only so much that local authorities can do at one time to develop a mixed economy. Further analysis showed that authorities which spent more on services for elderly people (per capita) were more likely to favour the establishment of not-for-profit trusts as an instrument of future policy, although London and metropolitan authorities tended to be less enthusiastic about this approach.

As we show in Chapter 7, the announcement in January 1991 that government guidance would be issued in April effectively caused planning blight. The position was not resolved until June 1991 when the Ministers for Social Security and Health announced that residents in homes transferred after 12 August would continue to be the financial responsibility of local authorities. For this reason, almost every effort to establish a trust was concentrating on residential facilities for adult client groups which might attract DSS funding: with no immediate financial pay-off, domiciliary and day care services were rarely mentioned.

In one authority, small local trusts already existed under consortium arrangements to support former long-stay hospital residents in the community. These trusts have one representative each from the local authority, health authority, a voluntary organization and a housing association. As the Director remarked, with dowry transfers and other sources of revenue, 'those [trusts] have considerable advantages; there is an element of joint funding being channelled into a single provider without even having a single purchasing function.'

If funding advantages encouraged authorities to float residential facilities out of the public sector, other factors discouraged complete privatization. Residents' security of tenure could be protected by licence agreements; local authorities could bring experience and expertise in managing housing projects; staff redundancies could be avoided; and authorities were less exposed if trusts collapsed. This last concern was voiced by many interviewees, although their choice of 'insurance' varied. Some sought to retain sufficient control to be able to bring services back into the authority if necessary; most favoured keeping a proportion of their facilities within their control. Cautious variants of these strategies were the decision by some authorities to float off only those facilities which accommodated less frail or dependent people, and a reluctance to decide on the proportion of facilities to be floated off until the social security status of residents had been clarified. The fear that the DSS might alter the eligibility rules after authorities had taken irreversible decisions was the most commonly voiced reservation about trusts. Other perceived difficulties related to the greater task of internal failure, financial uncertainties at the Housing Corporation, the cost of bringing local authority homes up to acceptable standards before housing associations could take them over, and simple politics. In a Labour authority, selling off local authority elderly people's homes was 'too sensitive...The Committee will be absolutely terrified. Imagine the newspaper headlines: "Labour authority sells off the elderly and makes a loss".' We examine this issue of residential home transfers and trusts in more detail in Chapter 7.

Management and staff buy-outs

Only seven authorities had *not* ruled out management or staff buy-outs, workers' cooperatives or employee share ownership schemes as possible supply options in the new mixed economy (Table 5.1), but in three authorities these options were simply among a number of supply arrangements being discussed, and in another, officers had not floated them as a practical idea and the Chair had not thought about them. In the event, no such arrangements were actually put in place in our sample authorities. Practical concerns included access to capital and general doubts about financial credibility and security. Members' main objections were that buy-outs were unethical and risked fraudulent and unfair practices. Such views were fostered by allegations of fraud in computing and other services sold to groups of staff elsewhere in the country. Ideological objections were also voiced: 'A management buy-out smacks rather more of a commercialist approach than a caring council's approach to floating off.' The most common reservation was that buy-outs did not appear to offer any guarantee of stability or security for clients, while lessening local authority control. As Flynn and Common (1990: 8) point out, 'it is not clear that this sort of arrangement will provide better care or more choice for users.' One Director, describing the situation in his authority, captured the views of many people:

> I think this authority's Conservatives are quite conservative with a small 'c'; I don't think they were ready for management buy-outs. I don't think the staff were ready for management buy-outs. There was absolute support and enthusiasm for the path we were taking on purchaser/provider split and care management, and I didn't want to ruin that with a dissident kind of concept which just would not have fitted the organization. So I didn't actually explore [buy-outs] very far.

Private and voluntary providers

There was generally little *active* encouragement of non-statutory suppliers. As we described in Chapter 4, there was marked local pride in authorities' own services, and attitudes to the voluntary sector were generally benign, although some social services Directors and Chairs were fairly dismissive when we canvassed their views on a significantly enhanced provider role for this sector. Attitudes to the private sector were more polarized. When financial or political imperatives made it impossible to resist pressures to shift the balance of provision away from the local authority, there was an overwhelming preference for semi-independent trusts as arrangements for providing social care which allowed local authorities to retain at least some degree of direct control. There are now fewer financial benefits from establishing such trusts, and local authorities' main activities in further developing a mixed economy of social care are the expansion of contracting-out and the tightening of financial and other links with non-statutory providers.

Service specifications and contracts

Contracting out has long been a feature of English social care services. Any local authority which has placed a child in a voluntary or private sector home or used foster placements has been using contracts of one form or another, and there are other examples of local authorities funding other agencies to provide social services on their behalf since at least the early years of the Century (Mencher 1958; Judge and Smith 1983; Brenton 1985; Knapp 1986). In the past, the 'contract' has usually been loosely specified, often taking the form of a general grant. One aim of the community care changes is to formalize, clarify and tighten the links between sectors. As one Director commented,

> The mixed economy is not new as far as we are concerned; we have been heavily into it for years and years. But what we have not been doing for years and years is clearly defining the service specifications; that's where the gap has been. We have heard that one facility will take X, so X goes there; but we're not sure to what extent that meets X's needs. That's where the difference will be.

Other than grants and contracts, local and central government use various means to stimulate or support non-statutory providers of social care, including staff secondments, use of buildings at zero or low rent, gifts of equipment, low interest loans, help with staff training, legal and administrative advice, tax relief for voluntary and some private providers (including non-domestic business rates, income tax and VAT) and demand-side subsidies (such as the social security payments for residential care in the non-statutory sectors which disappeared in April 1993). Contract funding, however, is now the fastest growing component of statutory sector support for non-statutory bodies (Knapp and Kendall 1991; National Council for Voluntary Organisations 1992b; Kendall and Knapp 1994).

Numerous rationales have been postulated for this support. The 1989 White Paper itself argued:

> Stimulating the development of non-statutory service providers will result in a range of benefits for the consumer, in particular: a wider range of choice of services; services which meet individual needs in a more flexible and innovative way; [and] competition between providers, resulting in better value for money and a more cost-effective service. (Secretaries of State 1989b: para. 3.4.3)

The White Paper also lauded the 'development work, advocacy, campaigning and education' activities of voluntary bodies (para. 3.4.14). These assumptions about the advantages of non-statutory providers are not particularly new (Webb and Webb 1912; Kramer 1981; Judge and Smith 1983; Knapp *et al.* 1990), but they remain largely untested. Many people and many authorities are sceptical about the benefits to them or their clients of using the private and voluntary sectors to provide social care services. Scepticism is not simply associated with political hue. On the right of the political spectrum, for example, are those who support changes which lessen the power and encroachment of the state, and on the left are those who welcome the emergence of small, participative community organizations which are serving minority or disadvantaged groups. Intermingled with these perspectives are other anticipated gains from contracting. It has been argued, for example, that contracting can take advantage of private expertise, cut costs, raise efficiency, pare down bureaucratic procedures, circumvent obstructive trade unions, by-pass political patronage, promote consumer choice, encourage specialization, increase the likelihood of innovative service arrangements and open opportunities for experiment without commitment.

Set against these putative advantages are various potential drawbacks, including the dangers of relations between non-government suppliers and government funders becoming a little too cosy, high administrative costs for both public and voluntary agencies, loss of autonomy by voluntary sector suppliers, employment insecurity and reductions in public sector accountability as money is pushed farther afield. As an alternative to non-specific grants, contracts have the advantages of clarity, predictability, a commitment to monitoring effectiveness and possibly financial security for suppliers; but, conversely, they are administratively more cumbersome, leave less room for innovation, risk-taking and flexibility, often move the practice emphasis from outputs to inputs and may actually work against rather than in support of efficiency improvements (Judge and Smith 1983; Kramer and Grossman 1987; Lipsky and Smith 1989; Gutch 1992).

Although we have drawn these postulated advantages and drawbacks from research conducted largely in the USA, many were also mentioned by our interviewees.

Identifying and stimulating providers

Most Directors and Chairs argued that it was too early for them to be soliciting bids for contracts actively, even assuming they were intending to take this route to a mixed economy. But the majority were consulting regularly with voluntary organizations, through the local council for voluntary service, via the grant-making process or through the complex interweaving of elected members and management boards. Few were holding similar discussions with private sector providers, as the KPMG (1992) survey subsequently also found. In some areas, seminars had been organized to explain or discuss community care plans, and a few model service specifications had been developed. None of this activity is yet particularly close to the formal mechanisms used in the USA to stimulate non-statutory suppliers: 'bidders' conferences, technical assistance, independent managerial advice funded by the public agency, aid in the creation of new agencies, and capital subsidies to cut the entry costs' (Kramer and Grossman 1987: 37). Active intervention of this kind is sometimes held to cut across the fundamental aims of a competitive tendering processes, and so is sometimes frowned upon, but activities to educate, encourage and assist potential providers, as well as purchasers, can be of considerable benefit.

Specifications and contracts

Although compulsory competitive tendering was introduced for some local and health services some years ago, including hospital catering, refuse collection, vehicle maintenance and school cleaning, it was not a component of the community care reforms. The government preferred to give

> local authorities an opportunity to make greater use of service specifications, agency agreements and contracts in an evolutionary way. The Government believes that this will have the beneficial effect of requiring authorities to define desired outcomes; to be more specific about the nature of the service they are seeking to provide to achieve those outcomes; and to define the necessary inputs. (Secretaries of State 1989b: para. 3.4.7)

A central task is the development of service specifications or agreements, which set out the quantity and quality of inputs and outcomes (for example, improvements in user welfare, the volume and standards of services, and care practices), target client groups, complaints and grievance procedures, monitoring and performance requirements, sub-contracting restrictions, renewal/termination processes and perhaps also an acceptable cost range. They set the need and policy contexts for service delivery. They may also make specifications regarding staff skills or qualifications, equal opportunities, user participation, the employment or serving of minority groups and even salary scales. Although bringing numerous advantages, the service specification can be cumbersome and demanding, particularly if users or carers are to be involved. For this reason, it is generally the case that less detailed service specifications are issued in the USA when more competition for contracts is expected, when the service needs of the population are less easily defined and when flexibility and responsiveness are essential. Whatever the level of detail, clarity is imperative. Contracts – the legal documents setting out agreements – cover the same dimensions as service specifications, with the addition of the agreed cost or unit price.

How, then, were local authorities responding to the government's suggestions that they introduce more formal service specifications? In all but a few authorities, service specifications, agreements or contracts were already in use or beginning to be developed. Broadly, there were five types of response.

The *floating voters* (four authorities) had simply not brought this aspect of the community care changes to the fore in the period between the Act (or perhaps since Griffiths) and our interviews in early 1991. Other changes had greater priority.

Two authorities could be described as *conscientious objectors*, having considered the arguments for tighter specifications and contracts, but rejected them. In one Conservative authority, both Director and Chair favoured a move to more service level agreements, although members were unconvinced. The embeddedness of the voluntary and private sectors within local authority decision-making structures – members of all political persuasions serve on management boards in most authorities – was a factor. One Labour authority had decided not to move towards contract specifications unless the present administration 'is still the government in four years time and they force us down that line...but I don't like doing it and I won't do it'.

The *new beginners* (six authorities, all Labour) had decided to use service specifications and contracts but had not yet introduced new arrangements. This was sometimes a question of timetabling, and sometimes a result of the gradual evaporation of opposition among officers or members, who had earlier been reluctant to discard successful grant-aid links. One Labour authority had used the voluntary sector for some specialist services – 'major placements for people with intensive needs on a fee-per-client basis' – and developed service level agreements with voluntary organizations for one client group – 'politically a highly contentious thing to do, but we were able to get away with it on the basis that the Department of Health were monitoring those grants quite precisely', as the Director described it. Members initially saw these developments as 'the thin end of the wedge...and certainly for some considerable time we [the officers] were not allowed to talk about service level agreements'. As the Chair in the same authority explained, at first he thought:

> This is taking us back decades, pre-local authority, pre-Seebohm; whereas I think the experience with the HIV work has enabled me to rethink it and to feel that maybe this is late twentieth-century social services after all...Looking back now at the success of the HIV contracts, I am very reassured. Also I suppose it makes you feel you can interpret all this legislation and all these guidance notes coming out of the DH imaginatively and creatively, and put your own stamp on it.

Nine *incrementalist* authorities had decided to expand their use of contracts, though carefully and relatively slowly. Typical of this approach was some gradual tightening of existing links with other agencies, but no issuing, at that stage, of new service specifications. Expansion of service specifications and contracts was anyway ruled out in some authorities if it implied contraction of public sector provision. The Director in one of these incrementalist authorities did not anticipate much change to the balance or level of payments to the voluntary or private sectors for a couple of years, although this would gradually change with increasing emphasis on 'our judgements of value for money'. He went on:

> If we don't think we can get value for money we're not going to use them. Or they are going to have to prove they can give us value for money. There will have to be measurements that we have not had before. For example, take a day care centre for twenty people. We're going to have to know who those twenty people are and how often they are attending to judge if we are getting reasonable value for money.

In a Labour authority which had traditionally been reluctant to support non-statutory services, except via a small number of grants, service level agreements were being moved forward cautiously, initially setting out the authority's expectations about equal opportunities policies, complaints procedures and staff training. At the next stage the authority wanted to raise quality issues and, later still, to introduce performance indicators to measure outcomes. The Director in a Conservative authority explained the reasons for the slow build up: 'It is being slowly developed. We're not worried about the havoc and chaos it might cause within the agencies. It's the speed at which our staff can get on with the task.'

Finally, three authorities were *proven enthusiasts*, having already drawn up service specifications or contractual links for many of their services. All were Conservative controlled. In one authority the Director told us how 'last year we entered into three-year agreements with the majority of organizations that were providing services for us and for the community'. Most grants in another authority had been replaced with service agreements, some to purchase particular services and some for advocacy work. The latter was often disguised by the officers from members ('The style of Conservatism here is that advocacy is a dirty word') by agreement on some core funds around which were draped payments for development of new functions and services. Three-year contracts had been set in place, with a minimum one year's notice of termination. Termination had just been decided for a large contract with one of the major day care providers because of what the local authority saw as excessively large overhead costs.

A fairly general opinion among authorities was that poor service agreements or contracts are those that which give providers immutable specifications, while better contracts allow scope for negotiation of both aims and the means to achieve them so as to build on the providers' strengths and expertise. A difficult balance must then be struck between clearly specifying the task and leaving scope for innovation and autonomy. There was no support for specifications or contracts which were too tightly drawn, although one Labour Chair rejected social care contracts altogether because they could not be specified tightly *enough*. Elsewhere, there was a desire for flexibility and trust:

> My own view is that the kind of Xshire model of specifying how many potatoes on a plate every day is the wrong way to go about it. You have

got to establish a set of quality standards and principles that you first ask potential contractors if they can meet, and then have some simple performance measures to indicate whether or not they are achieving those standards. Now you have got to be tighter than that, but I don't believe that you can specify care in the same way as you can specify how to resurface a road.

Another Director voiced similar reservations:

There are problems with competitive tendering and contracting in welfare. You can tie things down so tightly that if you don't have enough specification then people will find a way through it, and if you write a specification which is overtight they can't adhere to it and it becomes impossible to monitor. So we will probably be using general specifications of what we want, and doing business with people we have worked with before.

We looked for patterns of response among our sample authorities. It was interesting to find that authorities which had already introduced service specifications were those that previously devoted higher percentages of their spending on elderly people to grants and lower percentages to contracts. Early moves were often simply tightening up existing financial links. Lower spending authorities (per capita) tended to be less enthusiastic about service specifications and contracts.

Tendering procedures

The type of tendering – the degree and openness of competition that will be allowed or encouraged by local authorities – had not yet been decided by most authorities by early 1991, although a small number reported competitive tendering of one form or another. Thus, according to one Director of Social Services,

We were casting some bread upon the water to stimulate the development of services. What we're saying is: 'We're prepared to let some contracts which are worth this amount, come and bid and satisfy us you can do it.' And the common feature is a willingness to take a dollop of money and spend it in a different way and let the world know you are prepared to spend it in a different way...At the time that the Secretary of State pulled the rug [on the Community Care Act implementation timetable], we could have done contract specifications for residential care for the elderly, physically disabled and learning disabilities, and for domiciliary care and day care. We're tendering now for day care and domiciliary care; we have invited people to tender. We can't let contracts for residential care, so we have aborted that.

Taking advantage of the phased implementation, this authority was now looking at each of the agencies which had tendered for residential care in order to draw up a list of 'contractors designate' in which the authority had confidence. This same authority advertised widely for potential domiciliary care suppliers, invited them to complete questionnaires, and then invited a select group to tender for contract. This is an example of *select list tendering*, a process which permits only approved agencies to tender, there having been some earlier weeding out of agencies which do not look likely to meet quality, capacity or other requirements (Flynn and Common 1990). Price competition may or may not be a feature once the shortlist has been selected.

Another authority had used select list tendering to invite three voluntary agencies to tender for a children's rights officer, to stimulate offers to run a hostel and for some research work, but generally few authorities had reached a stage where they needed to introduce tendering. However, most had ideas about how they would be approaching the task when the time arrived.

Open competitive tendering, allowing anyone to make a bid, seems unlikely to be widely adopted, given the fears that it can emphasize cost criteria to the neglect of quality (Association of Metropolitan Authorities 1990), and bring social care contracts under the influence of the Local Government Act 1988, with its restrictions on non-commercial conditions. Many interviewees reported their authorities' unhappy experiences (in one case 'disastrous' experiences) with compulsory competitive tendering for other services. In one London borough most of the contracts were said to have collapsed, for example. In another, the Director believed that most of the competitive tenders had been 'rigged' to ensure that the authority won the contracts.

More common than compulsory competitive tendering are *single supplier negotiation* and *extant supplier negotiation* (not necessarily with a single agency), both of which might save administrative costs and cut the time needed to introduce contracts. By dealing with extant suppliers it is also possible to build service delivery insights into service specifications, further cutting costs and time, preserving continuity in service delivery, but perhaps unfairly favouring established agencies (so-called 'sweetheart' or 'insider dealing' arrangements). It is often not realized how deeply embedded in local power elites are some voluntary agencies (Seibel 1990). The voluntary sector connections of elected members and social care officials, all open, legal and in other circumstances to be welcomed, may not marry with the needs of (quasi-) competitive bidding for contracts. It was recognized that single supplier negotiation could reduce client choice, and thus work against one of the basic benefits of the care management model, even though it could offer economies of scale and cross-authority uniformity, and obviously potentially reduce administrative expenses. Too few authorities had clearly specified plans to be sure, but there was a general tendency for Labour authorities to favour single supplier tendering and for some Conservative authorities to look to bring competitive forces to bear. There was no discernible political control difference in the degree of preference for extant suppliers.

Voluntary or private suppliers?

In their study of social welfare contracts in the San Francisco Bay Area, Kramer and Grossman (1987) found a preference among government officials to award contracts to organizations which were larger and had longer track records, except when services were to be provided to particular ethnic groups. They also found a preference for voluntary over private agencies, though subject to cost and political influences. The same preference was evident among the local authorities in this study. Why might a local authority prefer to contract with a voluntary rather than a private agency?

Other things being equal, local authorities might prefer the supplier who comes closest to meeting their quality and quantity requirements at an affordable price. Given observable and easily monitored service and client outputs, and complete certainty as to the future behaviour of suppliers, the decision would be fairly straightforward. Rationales such as user choice, efficiency and innovation will come into play. But, as we argue in Chapter 6, social care is not like most other local government services, and if the decision is taken to contract with non-statutory organizations there often tends to be a preference for voluntary over private suppliers in circumstances where output is difficult to observe or measure. A voluntary body may engender more 'trust' because of the non-distribution constraint (profits cannot be distributed to owners) and it was apparently still widely feared that private sector bodies will 'shirk' on quality. Many voluntary organizations have service track records and good reputations extending back well before public or private (for-profit) provision. If, on the other hand, these uncertainty or transaction costs are outweighed by private sector price or efficiency, or better service quality, or a greater willingness to respond to public sector aims, the contract may go to the private sector. If, as is sometimes argued, private sector agencies can respond more rapidly to changing demand patterns (see, for example, Hansmann 1987), the service specification and contract negotiation stages may simply prove to be too short or the tasks too complex for the voluntary sector to make and win its case.

Contract type

Contracts can be of different kinds, the choice being dependent upon, among other things: the ease with which detailed specifications can be drawn up (related to the characteristics of services and their expected outcomes, and the amount of information already possessed by local authorities); the scale of contracting being contemplated; the administrative costs of reaching and monitoring agreements (many of which will not vary with the size of contract, and therefore will be comparatively more burdensome with small contracts); the incentive mechanisms to be built into the agreements, with the aim of containing costs, promoting good practice or whatever; the market structure and the degree of competition for contracts (the greater the monopoly or selling power of the suppliers, the tighter the contract specifications that would probably be needed); and the sector in which the supplier is located (private or voluntary).

Block contracts specify the facilities to be provided, and essentially allow a local authority to purchase access to facilities. Often they do not specify numbers of clients. These are administratively simple, input-focused contracts, but are inherently risky if they fail to specify quality. The incentive for the purchaser is to maximize use; the incentive for the supplier is to minimize costs, and one way to do this is to restrict usage, either overall or in relation to particular client types (the 'cream-skimming' problem). There is no obvious efficiency incentive operating on the supplier, but there is more scope for rapid responses to fluctuations in demand. Block contracts could simply replace one monopoly provider with another, and therefore tend to limit choice more than other contract forms, but 'could be highly appropriate where services are relatively self-contained and clearly defined' (Audit Commission 1992a: para. 77). A block contract with arrangements for care managers to 'call off' services in the fashion of 'spot' purchasing (see below) is one variant, but it shares most of the same disadvantages. The general grant to a voluntary organization is essentially a block contract, though with fewer specifications.

Cost and volume contracts specify the total cost or budget and the volume of service to be provided (the clients to be served) but not the welfare outcomes or quality of care. These latter need careful monitoring, as with any contract, but the purchaser will have less leverage over the supplier. Input or facility monitoring will not be specified. The drawback to the cost and volume contract is its 'very specificity': fewer services may actually be needed than those purchased in the contract, and money will therefore have been wasted, or there may be excess demand which the local authority will have to meet in some other way. Setting minimum and maximum limits can circumvent this problem.

Cost per case contracts pay an agreed amount per client or unit of output on delivery (retrospectively). 'Spot' purchasing by care managers is an example of this kind of contract, with purchases tailored to the needs of individual clients. Administratively they are the most costly for both purchasers and providers. Purchasers will want to set a ceiling on the number of clients or service outputs, or else they are likely to hit problems with open-ended commitments to fund demand-led care, while not reaping economies of scale. Purchasers will have the incentive to build flexibility into the contract (regarding client numbers and their service needs); suppliers will want to iron out costly fluctuations in the scale and need-variability of demand, and will probably want some guarantee of minimum income. Retrospective reimbursement is unlikely to enhance quality of care, and could well prove inflationary, if the US nursing home industry experience were to be repeated (Nyman 1985, 1988, 1990). If the nature of the service is not specified – that is, if reimbursement is based on numbers of clients with specified characteristics (effectively a *capitalization* funding method) – there is the incentive for contractors to choose the most profitable care packages, which may not be most beneficial for users or most cost-effective for society, and to resist service changes which involve new capital developments and other transitional costs.

Monitoring performance

Caring for People sets out the monitoring requirement on social services departments in broad terms:

> It will be essential that, whenever they purchase services, social services authorities should take steps to ensure that the quality to be delivered is clearly specified and properly monitored, bearing in mind that vulnerable people are involved as users. (Secretaries of State 1989b: para. 3.4.9)

The *quid pro quo* of local government funding of the private and voluntary sectors is performance monitoring. Compliance with the terms of contracts must be verified. The more specific the contract, the larger, but not necessarily the harder, the monitoring task. Monitoring is thus the ongoing oversight of contractors by funders, perhaps in the form of monthly or quarterly reports of, for example, client numbers and profiles, investment in staff training, or lengths of waiting lists. In the USA, as Kramer and Grossman (1987) report, monitoring is rarely used to provide an early warning of problems – the *compliance model* of regulation (Day and Klein 1987) – or even a steady flow of information for government planning. Monitoring is more likely either to be relatively routine or to follow the *deterrence model* – with the emphasis on punishment, that is, penalties and termination. Monitoring is also almost always defined in terms of inputs or process indicators – staff characteristics, room sizes, corridor widths, numbers of clients served, average length of stay, quality of inputs and so on. Evaluation, distinguished from monitoring as a longer-term, perhaps retrospective, appraisal of client welfare as related to the terms of the contract, 'is exceedingly rare and infrequently requested' (Kramer and Grossman 1987: 41; DeHoog 1985).

Why should monitoring and evaluation checks be needed at all? Aside from the fact that authorities retain statutory responsibility and also from the reasonable demands of financial probity where taxpayers' money is concerned, there is the problem that many clients of social care services are not in any position to judge quality or act upon their judgements. The market is not self-regulating. When there is excess demand for a service, users will also be disadvantaged in having restricted choice. The governance structures of private and voluntary organizations do not render them representative of consumers or citizens at large, and public agencies will be aware that non-statutory agencies may have their own ideas about the objectives of services and the means to achieve them, and that those ideas may not be acceptable when funded with public money. A decade ago, the regulatory procedures in place in Britain were seen as little more than minimal (Home Office statement in Wolfenden 1978; Hatch 1980; Kramer 1981; Judge and Smith 1983). This marginal influence was explained by Brenton (1985: 93) by 'the diminutive nature of the amounts [of public subsidies] involved from the government's point of view', the wish by public agencies not to counter the autonomy and flexibility of recipient bodies, and because close monitoring of all recipients is simply impracticable. One by-product from contract monitoring could be better appreciation by local authorities of their *own* services: aims, limitations, costs and qualities.

Renewing or terminating contracts

At the final stage in the contracting process, public agencies must decide whether to renew, modify or terminate a contract. There is likely to be strong bias in favour of contract renewal, not simply because the immediate costs of doing something tend to be higher than the costs of doing nothing. Established suppliers of complex services are further along their learning curves (it is hoped to the benefit of users, but almost certainly to the benefit of the suppliers themselves), competition from alternative potential suppliers may have disappeared during the period of the previous contract, political influence may be wielded by existing suppliers, suppliers can also mobilize user support, and public agencies probably follow the old cliché 'better the devil you know...'. Kramer and Grossman (1987: 43) quote a public agency director: 'I need the provider agency as much as they need me, so it's really almost impossible to terminate the inefficient contracts except where there is some dramatic case of malfeasance.' Paradoxically perhaps, this bias might *not* materialize in the UK in the early years of the new mixed economy, because some of the elected members on local authority social services committees may feel a need to flex their new muscle and terminate a few contracts. Whether this will generate an improved supply response (in terms of better quality services) or simply lose potential suppliers remains to be seen. And of course the ultimate sanction of contract termination can only be applied if there is another and better supplier waiting to move in.

Competition and choice

It is clear from the findings reported in this chapter that, although the NHS and Community Care Act places a requirement on local authorities to develop a mixed economy of provision, few authorities are currently thinking in market terms or have developed plans to promote competition. In early 1991, only six of our twenty-four sample authorities were working to develop or encourage markets. These tended to be authorities which already devoted high proportions of their total social services spending to grants and contracts, and they were also more likely to be Conservative controlled. We now turn to the prospects for social care markets.

6

Social care is different

Introduction

The government anticipates that pluralism in social care provision will enable specialist and innovative practices to emerge, and that competition will enhance choice and cost-effectiveness. In principle, a local authority that has to choose the providers with which it will do business should prefer those which come closest to meeting its quality and quantity requirements at an affordable price. Given observable and easily monitored service and client outcomes, and certainty about the future behaviour of providers, the choice would be straightforward. But these ideal conditions seldom apply in social care. Few people anticipate competition between alternative providers of the kind waged up and down the High Street by retailers and supermarkets. Social care 'commodities' have numerous features which may render them unsuitable to an unfettered, unregulated market. Social care, it is often said, is *different*.

The two previous chapters described local authorities' broad attitudes and responses to legislative change and central guidance, and the actions taken to introduce or extend a mixed economy of social care. What are the incentives and impediments that could influence the future direction or pace of development?

Local authorities are more likely to express enthusiasm for a mixed economy when:

- the perceived cost savings, quality improvements and choice options are greater;

- the fiscal pressures are felt to weigh more heavily; and
- there is strong political or ideological support for this broad policy direction.

Whether the mixed economy envisaged by the present government can deliver cost effectiveness, quality improvements and enhanced choice may well depend on the ability of market forces to operate freely and fairly. This chapter considers markets and local authorities' expectations concerning them, and discusses the implications for cost, quality and choice. These are all efficiency criteria, so it is important that we also consider the implications of the new mixed economy for equity. First, the fiscal pressures facing authorities and their implications for resources are examined, and then the underlying ideological stances which can create incentives and disincentives to develop a mixed economy are considered.

At the time of the fieldwork there was also externally generated political and policy uncertainty about: whether local government structures as a whole would be radically altered after the 1992 general election; whether local authorities would continue to have lead responsibility for community care; and whether, even if they did have this responsibility, they would be required to accelerate the diminution in their service-providing function and promote a mixed economy through compulsory competitive tendering. It should be said, however, that although commonly viewed as underlying anxieties, these collectively represented not so much a tangible obstacle to the development of a mixed economy, as a constraining or debilitating context. These concerns, expressed in ten sample authorities, were not sufficient wholly to impede what authorities were doing: the effect, rather, was to sap morale and lessen the enthusiasm with which they might otherwise seek to implement change.

Fiscal pressures

About half of all local authority expenditure is now funded from revenues raised locally from the council tax, from investments or from fees charged to service users. While this proportion has grown since the late 1970s, the opportunity for central government control of local action has also become considerable (Rhodes 1992). Central government has used these controls as instruments of economic and public policy. Many of the fiscal constraints on English local authorities are thus externally determined, and it is clear that they are having far-reaching implications for social care policies and practices. The constraints are not only encouraging the diversification of funding and provision, but are also potentially impeding it.

A number of interrelated resource factors were identified by interviewees as incentives to promote a mixed economy. The first priority for many authorities, as described in more detail in the next chapter, was to address issues surrounding their residential services. In particular, a large proportion of their stock was considered to be of a standard that would be unacceptable if found in the private or voluntary sector. Tight limits on capital expenditure meant that many authorities lacked the resources to upgrade such homes. *Caring for People* affected this situation in two ways. First and most clearly, it provided through the income support rules a further disincentive for local authority provision. Second, it ensured that once arm's-length inspection units became operational, the general discrepancies between non-statutory and some public provision would be manifest.

A number of Directors and Chairs were blunt about the nature of the income support 'incentive' for diversification of public sector provision; an incentive, moreover, by which local authorities were differentially disadvantaged in comparison to private and voluntary sector providers (the sloping, not level, playing field). As one (Conservative) Chair said,

> Let's be quite honest. The reason for considering a not-for-profit trust is because of the government's funding policy, and make no bones about that. The whole point is that if an elderly person is resident in our homes we have to pick up the tab, whereas if they go into the private sector, they can get income support and DSS money. So that's a big influence on one's policy.

According to one Director, it was the severity of the pressures which had caused members to 'bite the bullet' of encouraging alternatives to public sector provision.

Financial pressures were also obstacles to change, referred to by either the Director or Chair in virtually every one of our sample authorities (Table 6.1). One commented that 'the main obstacle is money...inadequate funding or funding at the wrong time and in the wrong place.'

There was widespread doubt or scepticism among both officers and members in 1991 about whether social security funds would be transferred to local authorities in 1993 and, if they were, whether they would be sufficient. There was equally widespread concern that without ringfencing there could be no guarantee that social services departments would actually receive all of the transferred funds. In the face of such financial uncertainty, authorities argued that they could not advance their discussions with alternative providers.

Resource scarcity had put particular limits on new developments in *information technology* (IT) and staff training. The Department of Health's policy guidance stressed the need for authorities to match financial control and information systems to the new enabling structure, but the inability to do precisely this matching was cited as a significant obstacle in a third of authorities (compare Audit Commission 1992a: paras 40–43; Hoyes *et al.* 1991: Chapter 4). One Director explained that his authority 'has a very clear IT plan, which is related to our need for information systems, but the prospect of ever getting it up and running is pretty remote because of our financial position.' Without the necessary investment in information systems and technology it is difficult to see how authorities will be able to make the best use of care management, devolved budgeting, needs-led planning, authority-wide outcome monitoring or proper costings on which to base contract specifications: 'The major piece

of work that has to be done in this authority is in terms of thinking through
the financial infrastructure to take on board care management. The information
bases aren't there because we've got no IT whatsoever.' Much the same view
was reported in other authorities, and the funds made available by the government for investment in improved IT systems were widely described as inadequate when compared to the sums made available to both health authorities
and education departments. Moreover, it was an inauspicious time for authorities to be using their own resources. Three of the eight Directors who had
identified IT deficiencies as an obstacle to the development of a mixed economy
remarked that members took a dim view of such an investment at a time
when they were cutting services.

The policy guidance emphasized the need for *staff training* strategies to
develop new skills. A number of authorities referred to the inadequacy of
training budgets or cited shortages of management expertise among senior
staff (notably in areas such as contract specification and negotiation), and
shortages of the skills necessary for care management (Table 6.1). In relation
to the latter, one Director expressed his concern that

> We are not going to have enough professionally competent workers to do
> those sophisticated assessments. [The result would be] poor quality assess-

Table 6.1 Local authorities' perceived obstacles to change

Perceived obstacle	Number of authorities identifying this obstacle as an important problem
Political/policy uncertainty	10
Money; financial pressures	22
Inadequate information technology/systems	11
SSD staff skills shortages	7
Social services staff resistance	6
Mistrust of the private sector	9
Unwillingness to consider some alternative providers	11
Paucity of alternative suppliers	9
Changing view of the caring role of families	3
Labour market changes	4
Underdevelopment of alternative suppliers	13
Paucity of volunteers	8
VAT payments by private and voluntary organizations	1
High land and property prices facing providers	2
Rural premium on costs	4
Voluntary agencies unwilling to develop as providers	8
LA anxiety about loss of control	4
Disjunction of LA and NHS reform timetables	7
Total number of authorities sampled	24

ments, poor quality decisions and people ending up in the wrong systems – which is going to be a damn sight more expensive.

The financial strains on local authorities in recent years have also left their mark on the voluntary sector. Local authority funding of the sector as a whole has never been particularly large, averaging just 1 per cent of total spending during the 1980s (Mocroft 1991), but showed a significant decline in 1991/92, with further reductions in prospect for 1992/93 (Mabbott 1992). The largest reductions were in urban areas. Within this declining sum, grants were gradually giving way to fees. Ironically, however, the local authority interviewees were also describing how financial constraints were limiting their expected ability to monitor contracts and providers.

Ideological influences

The *Policy Guidance* noted that

> implementation will require substantial changes in the role and approach of staff at all levels in the health service and personal social services...there is a need for changes in attitude and culture throughout agencies commissioning and providing care. (Department of Health 1990a: para. 1.19)

A fundamental component of the recent legislative changes in community care – as outlined in Chapters 1 and 2 – is the move away from the local authority as dominant provider. In this respect, there has been a collective mind shift at senior level: 'The writing is very clearly on the wall for local government...I see less and less prospect of us being able to be heavily the major (service) provider.' None the less, it is important to repeat the point made in Chapter 4 that, however widespread the acceptance of this general trend, and however willingly or unwillingly accepted, there was an equally widespread belief that local authorities both will and should remain significant service providers. This view, born in part of a straightforward pride in public sector provision, was not restricted to Labour-controlled authorities:

> Social services has never taken an active part in the corporate development of policy in [this authority]. It has always been seen as the 'wet' bit of the local Conservative approach where the caring old buggers sit on the social services committee, and by and large the key members do not interfere and are not greatly interested in social services activities. As long as we keep them out of the newspapers and don't cause them too many problems in their surgeries then they are happy for us to trundle on.

This stance is linked to another commonly held view that part of this ideological change is an acceptance that SSDs must increasingly identify and focus upon a set of core activities.

As we reported in Chapter 5, only six authorities in 1991 unambiguously and enthusiastically subscribed to the market approach to the delivery of social care. Despite the government emphasis on local authorities being able to achieve greater value for money via their commissioning roles within a more competitive market, few people identified this as sufficient incentive for promoting a mixed economy. Many more, however, adduced greater client choice as a genuine incentive. The Director in a Conservative authority spoke for many in describing his authority's approach:

> Members are very keen on the idea of service delivery being to the best advantage of the user. If that's in-house, jolly good. Mind you, it's got to be cost-effective to survive here. If it's independent, that's equally good, but it has to be of a good quality...Members are quite happy to run all our services in-house: they certainly don't want to put them out for the hell of it. They haven't got that sort of political imperative. But equally, they don't want to be running inefficient services when someone else outside could do it better. So we have – which is I think what the government wanted – a genuine approach to the mixed economy based on the best interests of users at the most affordable cost.

These ideological changes have not spread throughout social services departments or committees, where staff or members may be reluctant to give up their provider role and accept the mixed supply of care. Thus, for example, Chairs in two Labour-controlled councils referred to the distance between their own views and those of their colleagues. One saw the enabling role – with its clearer focus on user choice and the setting and control of standards – as being not in itself antithetical to a history of municipal socialism, but noted that colleagues regretted such a change of role as a betrayal of that tradition. There was commonly a noticeable difference between senior social services managers and others, with the former more readily accepting the new enabling role for local authorities. As one Director said of his staff, 'It is a difficult issue for certain professionals to take on because there are those who are committed to a welfare state role and who find it extremely difficult and a complete culture change to be talking about buying in services.'

Ignorance, misunderstanding and mistrust between local authorities and the private sector were widespread and mutual. Such antagonism was referred to by private sector representatives, and acknowledged by some Directors and Chairs. Private sector providers saw the antagonism emanating from local authority members, and from middle managers and fieldwork staff. Some of the antagonism represented a simple difference of view about the legitimacy of any role for the private sector in the provision of social care, associated with straightforward ideological differences and municipal pride (see Chapter 4), as well as the perception that the profit motive was incompatible with social care. These concerns are, according to the Audit Commission (1992a: para. 50), 'understandable, if misplaced'. The private sector obviously had its own interpretations: 'It is a political attitude which says private sector is bad; we won't put anybody in there if we can avoid it...It's at the sharp end, the junior manager, the potential community care manager...that we hear all these unfortunate statements.' One Chair of social services echoed this concern: 'There is a reluctance on the part of some people – not senior management but middle management – to do deals with the private sector; and it's a difficult one because they are the people who are responsible for making it work.'

The apparent misunderstanding and, less frequently, the mistrust of the private sector by local authorities often seemed to be based on ignorance of motives and attitudes, partly due to the traditional distance between the sectors in the planning process. (Arguably, this misunderstanding and mistrust of the private sector today mirrors local authorities' views about the voluntary sector a decade ago.) As we have indicated previously, local authority maps of suppliers vary in quality and definition: generally complete for private sector residential provision, because authorities are responsible for registration, and often detailed for much voluntary sector provision – domiciliary and day care included – because authorities either make grants to the agencies or fund councils for voluntary service to compile directories. However complete the map, knowledge of voluntary sector (and not-for-profit) provision will generally be fuller not only because many local authority members and officers are represented on voluntary organizations' committees but also because the voluntary sector has for some years had representation, as of right, on the formal joint planning machinery of joint consultative committees and joint care planning teams.

The private sector, by contrast, has rarely had such representation. Now, however, following publication by the government of a ministerial directive (Department of Health 1993c), local authorities will be required as part of the community care planning process to show that planning agreements are the product of a partnership between all other relevant parties – including the private sector. Previously, as most Directors accepted, private sector suppliers have been excluded from local service planning and design. In a minority of cases this exclusion was deliberate, but in most cases it was said to be because private sector proprietors had never sought to become involved. When asked whether this represented positive discouragement, most Directors contended that it was simply that they had not been approached: a case of inactive rather than active exclusion. Subsequent work by KPMG Management Consultants (1992) gives a fuller picture of non-statutory sector involvement (or not) in the first round of community care plans (1992/93). The report discusses the reasons for the low degree of involvement of the private sector especially.

The cultural change in local authorities should not be underestimated, but this has been less of a Damascene ideological conversion than a pragmatic response to cumulative fiscal pressures. There are fewer born-again free marketeers to be found among social services officers and members than disgruntled dabblers in service specifications and contracts. As we illustrate time and again in this book, most of the local authority respondents, including Conservative members, were strongly of the opinion that *social care is different* – that the culture of the market has limited relevance. The reasons for this need to be understood if authorities are to make appropriate use of, and develop, the mixed economy.

Market successes and drawbacks

Local authorities showed more enthusiasm for a mixed economy of care when they saw clear advantages flowing from it in terms of cost savings, quality and outcome improvements, and the enhancement of user choice. Most of the local developments observed since 1990 can be explained in this way. But authorities were and remain much less sanguine about the benefits of *markets*. Is market-style competition an achievable objective for social care?

There are two basic issues. The first is whether a local authority can accept the values, principles and ethics of the market place. Will it engage in hard-nosed price negotiation? Will it be prepared to draw up detailed contract specifications and conduct the close monitoring which many of these could entail? Will it initiate public sector redundancies if in-house provision is to be reduced? Will it let some private sector residential and nursing homes go out of business? Will it stand by and allow long-established traditional voluntary sector agencies to struggle and disappear? Evidence from elsewhere, particularly the USA, is congruent with the observation that local authorities reveal greater enthusiasm for market mechanisms when the fiscal pressures upon them are greater, and of course when their own ideological positions are more attuned to a market culture. The encouragement of markets is also more likely when authorities perceive them as offering significant local quality, cost or choice improvements. This raises the second issue. Do local authorities have the expertise to use markets to their, and their users', best advantage, while offering a fair deal to providers?

Under certain conditions, markets will succeed in producing socially efficient allocations of services,[1] but there are also numerous potential difficulties. The most likely stumbling blocks can be grouped under the three heads of structural imperfections, 'product' variability and information imperfections.[2]

Structural imperfections

The problem of *structural imperfections* occurs when market power can be wielded by one or more purchasers or providers. A possibility voiced by many people is that few social care markets will contain enough actual or potential purchasers or providers to prevent these structural imperfections arising. One of the exceptions will be residential and nursing home care for elderly people, where there is clearly a marked excess supply in some parts of the country. When there is excess demand, the result could be that price, service orientation, quantity and quality will be determined by one or a small group of incumbent agencies. These agencies will select those configurations which better suit them (and their profit margins, or modes of operation, and so on), safe in the knowledge that their position is unlikely to be credibly challenged or threatened. However, their selections may not particularly benefit service users.

The creation and development of a mixed economy that produces the cost reductions, quality improvements and broadening of choice which the government is seeking thus depends upon an adequate number and range of alternative suppliers of services. But there already appears to be a number of limiting though not mutually exclusive factors:

• the number of alternative suppliers;
• the ability of these suppliers to assume a larger or different service-providing role;
• the ease with which new suppliers can gain entry to the market; and
• the willingness of existing and new suppliers to agree to the contractual links which will be an important part of the new mixed economy.

Too few suppliers

It was a widely held view among the people we interviewed in local authorities that there is no sizeable, vibrant non-statutory sector ready and willing to take on a larger service-providing role, particularly in relation to domiciliary, day and respite care. Today's private and voluntary sectors, they argued, are unable to supply sufficient quantities of services of the requisite standard to replace local authority provision. Many social services directors were seeking to stimulate provision. (This was not, however, the primary reason for some local authorities transferring residential homes from the public to the not-for-profit sector, or selling them to private agencies. See Chapter 7.) In the longer term, of course, excess demand could allow providers to earn greater profits (or greater freedom of manoeuvre in other areas), attracting new providers to the market. Only if there are high entry barriers – for example, if new service providers have to invest heavily before they can operate economically – or if information imperfections are severe will the paucity of providers persist.

In many localities, the voluntary sector is largely composed of traditional small-scale agencies active in campaigning, lobbying and advocacy, or providing services (such as luncheon clubs). Obviously there are exceptions, but generally these cover local branches of national voluntary organizations, such as Age Concern (which makes a substantial contribution in many localities to day care provision), Mind and Mencap (which provide a wide variety of residential and non-residential services), and the WRVS and Crossroads. Even though widespread, these organizations are not ubiquitous. Moreover, particularly in the case of organizations whose branches are autonomous, there is no unanimity of opinion among local branches that they should take on a larger service-providing role in contractual relationships with local authorities. 'Philanthropic insufficiency', as Salamon (1987) has termed it, is a pervasive constraint, and the voluntary sector could remain a minor and fragmented player.

A danger associated with a paucity of suppliers is that local authorities might try to encourage either new agencies or the considerable expansion of one or two existing bodies by offering large block contracts. This approach runs the risk of replacing monopolistic local authority provision with monopolistic voluntary or private provision. The disadvantage could be service uncertainty, lack of control and high barriers to entry because of economies of scale. Of course, if the local authority is the single or main purchaser – which is more likely in remote areas than in conurbations, and for certain non-specialist services – it will be in a strong position to influence price and/or quality. Bilateral monopoly may not be so damaging if supplier behaviour can be influenced by user 'voice' (as opposed to 'exit') in addition to the local authority's countervailing monopsony power.

The Department of Health issued its statutory directive on user choice in December 1992. The directive encourages local authorities to look more favourably on spot purchasing rather than block contracts, although the government has also assumed that authorities can use their bulk purchasing strength to fill the 'care gap'. Structural imperfections might still develop as small and once-autonomous providers collude or merge in order to strengthen their bargaining positions vis-à-vis purchasers. One of the major trends in the internal organizational structure of voluntary agencies in the US social welfare sector is the tendency that 'the bigger organizations get bigger and the smaller organizations get bigger' (Kramer 1988: 11). The potential is there for market power to develop and to be abused, coupled with the lurking dangers of increased bureaucratization, formalization and goal deflection.

Underdeveloped suppliers

Two common perceptions among local authorities were that the infrastructures of most small local voluntary organizations could not cope with the demands of the new mixed economy, and that private agencies had neither the skills nor the inclination to diversify from residential care. Many of the local authority interviewees in 1991 questioned the ability of these organizations to develop a major new service-providing role without considerable investment in staff recruitment, training, management and financial accounting systems. Few interviewees were as blunt as the Director who remarked that 'the vast bulk of the voluntary sector is very weak organizationally; it's a shambles'. However, a number of other Directors and Chairs echoed his view that 'there are a small number of well-organized voluntary bodies which are primarily run by means of the local authority: every time I go to an AGM of a voluntary body, half my staff are sat on the management committee.'[3]

Evidence on non-profit child welfare organizations in Massachusetts emphasizes the existence of different types of organization, some well placed to succeed in the contract market (Lipsky and Smith 1989). Unfortunately, some of the voluntary organizations which English local authorities might want to encourage to take new or enhanced roles – such as those serving people from ethnic minorities – are often the least well prepared (National Council for Voluntary Organisations 1990; Kendall and Knapp 1994).

Private suppliers might be attracted into the market by the prospect of profits, but if local authorities wish to encourage new *voluntary* suppliers, they may themselves have to provide seed-corn money to recruit and develop the necessary expertise. The 'Catch 22' for the local authority could be its reluctance to enter into a contractual relationship with a supplier it regards as managerially unskilled to fulfil the contract, set against its reluctance to use its discretionary resources – if indeed it has them – to develop such managerial competencies. The Catch 22 for the voluntary organization is that it may not want to enter into contracts without this expertise, yet it may be unable to attract the necessary expertise until it has negotiated contracts and the attendant income.

Barriers to entry

When there are too few suppliers – or when current suppliers are not meeting the price, quantity or quality demands of purchasers – the frictionless working of a readily contestable market would encourage the entry of new suppliers. Reports of high profit margins or comfortably secure positions of current suppliers would attract them in. (When there are too *many* suppliers, some will go out of business or will be forced to diversify, as has happened with residential child care since 1949.)

New suppliers may not be able to compete on equal terms with existing suppliers, however. It may take a long time or prove costly to enter the market. (Gronbjerg 1990 describes how proposals for social welfare contracts in Chicago were usually required within three or four weeks of announcement, yet had to include complex specifications and budgets.) Smaller non-statutory agencies may find the administrative overheads of contract bidding and negotiation excessive, may not have access to national infrastructural support or expertise, and may not easily win the confidence of purchasers. Potential new providers may not have ready access to venture capital, and yet may face considerable 'sunk costs'. In these circumstances, existing suppliers have clear advantages over potential suppliers. In contracting, short lead times, complex service specifications, acquired knowledge of a local authority's preferences and demands, experience as to one's own best service responses, reputation, visibility and embeddedness within decision-making processes combine to aid the incumbent supplier. Although one of the sample authorities had invited tenders for domiciliary services so as to create a level playing field, a number of authorities had already decided to invite bids only from extant suppliers. Possession – 'first mover advantage' – may be nine-tenths of the law.

A further disincentive could be fabricated by existing suppliers. They could keep profit margins low and inconspicuous by underpricing their services, and then hike them up later if there are high transaction costs and low client turnover rates. For example, moving frail elderly people between different residential care homes endangers their welfare, and perhaps their lives, giving unscrupulous suppliers a fairly wide margin for manoeuvre in the pursuit of larger pecuniary gains. An increase in profits achieved by leaving fees unaltered and cutting expenditure will usually eventually result in poorer quality care, but may go undetected in the short term because many clients are not vocal and do not have the power of exit, and because outputs are hard to measure and monitor (characteristics to which we return below).

New providers, or current providers seeking to expand, could face re-source supply constraints. Some of the resources on which they rely in order to deliver a service which is distinctive are not readily available, or at least not at the same price. An obvious constraint relates to *volunteers*, both those sitting on the committees of voluntary organizations and those actually deliver-ing services. One local authority Director remarked that 'the idea that the whole world is out there full of enterprising business people who want to run voluntary bodies is rubbish'.

There are many possible explanations (Knapp 1990; Lynn and Davis Smith 1991). In many parts of one shire county, the WRVS 'can't get volun-teers to do more than two days a week [delivering meals on wheels]'. An Age Concern organizer feared that private and not-for-profit domiciliary and day care services might attract volunteers away with the offer of salaried employ-ment.

Private social care providers rely much less on volunteers, and so may not be restricted from entering the market, but many are dependent on the long hours and low rate of remuneration of proprietor-managers, and the uncosted inputs of family members (Judge and Knapp 1985). Such low-cost resources typical of the small family enterprise are not available in abundance. Because of European Community directives, small private (or voluntary) domi-ciliary care agencies must pay VAT on carers' wages, as well as on the administration of the services provided, when the VAT registration threshold amount (currently £35,000) is reached (National Council for Voluntary Organisations 1992a). One social services Director thought that this legislation 'will frustrate any major development of an alternative welfare state in domi-ciliary and day care'. An added complication is that some grants, tax exemptions and support in kind subsidize the voluntary but not the private sector, which may well help to compensate the former for the difficulties faced in raising venture capital, but which also simply distorts competition (Hansmann 1987, 1989; Weisbrod 1989).

Willingness to accept contracts
A fourth limiting factor could be that voluntary and private agencies may not be willing to take on or increase a service-providing role under the contractual arrangements offered by local authorities. Voluntary organizations are par-ticularly concerned about a number of issues.[4] The objectives set out by a local authority's service specification may not be in consonance with an organization's mission; indeed a charity is bound by the objectives in its trust instrument, constitution or memorandum of association (Gutch 1991; War-burton and Morris 1991). The more specific the service specification and

contract, the better the chances of public sector accountability, but the greater the potential loss of autonomy and the administrative and monitoring costs, and the lower the chances of innovative, efficient service packages emerging.

Voluntary bodies may not be able to pursue their campaigning or advocacy activities with the same energy, either because their attentions are diverted to managing contracts or because their contracts forbid it. They may not feel able fully to involve users in decision-making (or they may be forced to do so when they would otherwise not have done). Their volunteer management committees may become marginalized as increasingly complex agreements are established. Voluntary organizations may have to compete with one another for contracts, thus straining or even destroying mutual support networks built up over many years. Even the main benefit of contracts often identified for voluntary and private organizations – greater security of funding – is less a consequence of contracts as such than the result simply of thinking seriously about the difficulties that these organizations have always faced. The benefit appears to have been exaggerated (National Council for Voluntary Organisations 1991; Gutch 1992).

Product heterogeneity

A second source of market failure is *variability or heterogeneity of product*. If different people have needs or preferences for different types of service, and if providers can differentiate their products by adjusting their characteristics or quality, the provider can acquire market power. They will be able to influence or even control both price and quality. They could use their market power to choose the types of client served, in particular the 'creaming' of 'easier', less dependent users whose care will cost less. Voluntary organizations often, it is argued, meet the demand for differentiated products (see Weisbrod 1977; James and Rose-Ackerman 1986), and may resist attempts to change their product characteristics to those required by local authority purchasers, as doing so may be seen as distortion of their missions. Unlike private sector providers, increasing the rewards (payments) for these products will not necessarily induce voluntary providers to make product changes (Lipsky and Smith 1989).

Thus, on the one hand, the needs for many care services are simply too diverse and particular relative to the economically viable level of supply for there to emerge in most areas more than two or three providers. The first source of market difficulties – the structural imperfections – suggests that there may be too few providers for market forces to work to the benefit of purchasers and users. The second potential problem – product heterogeneity – suggests that providers, whether few or many in number, might be able to influence the price, characteristics and quality of the service. Hence, the simple desire for price competition which appears to lie behind the community care reforms would be misplaced. There is, in fact, a tension between encouraging sufficient service diversity so as to offer users a choice, while at the same time hoping that the diversity is not so marked that it allows providers to exploit users' heterogeneous preferences to gain the market power to control prices.

If there are numerous high-quality providers of a reasonably homogeneous product, there will be validity in the government's claim that local authorities will be able to negotiate on favourable price terms, create pressure for efficiency and effectiveness, and lessen the chances of the abuses that come from market power. But in other circumstances, such as in the delivery of the kinds of specialist care for which parts of the voluntary sector are renowned, competition will be waged in terms of service characteristics and quality as well as price: the seller's market.

Is this form of market failure likely to arise in social care? Quality competition is particularly important with third party reimbursement – for example, social security payments or local authority contracts[5] – as evidenced by US health care markets (Joskow 1983; Robinson and Luft 1985; Nyman 1985, 1989; Dusansky 1989; Maynard 1991). In English residential child care services in the early 1980s, both price and quality were set by voluntary sector providers. Price competition was more important for the comparatively large number of 'non-specialist' community homes than for the specialist facilities, such as homes with educational facilities for disabled children (Knapp 1986). There was a degree of price-responsiveness among authorities: a 10 per cent increase of voluntary home fees relative to local authority costs generated, on average, a 6 per cent fall in the proportion of an authority's residential child care population placed in voluntary homes (Knapp and Forder 1993).

Information imperfections

When some or all parties involved in a market transaction are ignorant of the values of key parameters such as price or quality, there are *information imperfections*. They will distort competition, and are likely to be rife in markets for services with outcomes which are uncertain, technically complex, infrequently produced, of long gestation, and embodied in the characteristics of users. Social care services are 'experience goods' because information on quality becomes available only after use (Nelson 1970). An associated complication is the asymmetric distribution of information. Providers will often start with more information about the service than purchasers, although over time the latter will acquire better information about providers, their products and consequences for users, allowing them to write contracts which embody incentives to good practice, high quality and efficiency. Transaction costs for purchasers should gradually fall. Indeed, if the threat of contract termination is credible, if alternative suppliers are available and if user feedback is reliable, the transaction costs of monitoring could be low. These circumstances might pertain, for example, in residential care services for elderly people.

In these circumstances, the nature and outcome of market interactions could be changed fundamentally because providers have an incentive to misrepresent their private information. The purchaser will have to bear the cost of collecting this information, or risk being exploited (Williamson 1975, 1985; Walsh 1989; Kendall 1991). These *transaction costs* could be high in the future mixed economy of social care. Client purchasers have usually had little relevant 'market' experience, have few opportunities or are less well positioned to voice their opinions (owing to service complexity or individual disabilities). They cannot make a credible threat of 'exit' because they cannot easily move their custom from one provider to another without considerable personal risk (Vladeck 1980). However, we must not fall prey to selective myopia, for there will always be transaction costs associated with local authority provision, albeit probably somewhat smaller. When hidden or denied, there can be unfortunate consequences for standards and users.

These transaction costs could mean that purchasers – whether they are users, care managers or local authority senior officers – will prefer certain types of provider to others. In choosing a non-statutory contractor, there are numerous reasons why a local authority might prefer a voluntary supplier to a private organization (Hansmann 1980; Krashinsky 1986). There is, for example, a common preference for voluntary over private suppliers in circumstances where the monitoring of service quality and outcomes is difficult. The voluntary body engenders greater trust because it is ruled by the constraint that profits cannot be distributed to owners. Competition also means losers as well as gainers. The commercial collapse of a non-statutory provider will damage user welfare, and have potentially enormous political consequences. These concerns were commonly voiced by local authority interviewees. Other reasons were given for having greater confidence in the voluntary sector. Many voluntary organizations have long track records and good reputations as successful innovators and expert providers. Many have encouraged user participation in management for a long time, helping to ensure that service quality is not impaired. Voluntary sector management boards not only often appear to share the philosophies of local authorities, but also frequently have several local authority officers among their number.

Experience in the USA could stoke local authority anxieties about information imperfections. Contract monitoring which concentrates on inputs or simple service features presents providers with the opportunity to obey the letter of the contract but not the incentive to pursue any additional margin of excellence (Flynn and Common 1990). A study of Wisconsin nursing homes found greater compliance with input and simple service regulations by private homes when compared with voluntary facilities, but a greater frequency of resident complaints in the former (Weisbrod and Schlesinger 1986). If those complaints reflect resident welfare, albeit imperfectly, this is a good illustration of the reasons for anxiety.

Of course, if the transaction costs of working with the private sector are outweighed by its comparative efficiency, better service quality or greater willingness to conform to local authority specifications, it could be chosen as the preferred provider. The probability of low transaction costs will be greater for services whose outcomes are more tangible or less complex, are targeted at needs which display less variability across the population and are not part of a policy to effect substantial redistributions of resources or welfare. The trade-off between efficiency and control will be determined in part by fiscal conditions and political forces.[6]

Cost, quality, choice and equity

What are the prospects for cost, quality, choice and equity as market forces play an increasingly large part in the developing mixed economy of social care? And what implications are there for local authority roles?

Cost

The fiscal pressures faced by local authorities will undoubtedly encourage them to seek arrangements for commissioning and provision which keep costs at a reasonable level, and which conceivably force them down. Cost reduction is widely touted by pro-marketeers as a desirable consequence of the reforms, and it is not hard to find evidence of cost differences between statutory and non-statutory services. However, there are reasons for believing that these cost reductions may not be large or easy to obtain.

An obvious difficulty will arise if the new markets for social care are characterized by the kinds of structural imperfections which put power into the hands of profit-seeking suppliers. A number of potential barriers to entry to social care markets have been identified. There is also the danger that local authorities will enter into block contracts with monopsonistic suppliers who might pare their prices to the bone in the short term in confident expectation of the opportunity to widen profit margins in two or three years' time. Authorities should thus be wary of favouring existing providers over new entrants. On the other hand, local authorities which choose to enter into contracts with a multiplicity of providers could lose the opportunity to gain from economies of scale in contract negotiation, monitoring and production. Transaction costs associated with contract drafting, monitoring and enforcement could be especially significant for complex services used by people who have few opportunities or abilities to voice their opinions of quality, or where the user outcomes are intangible or of long gestation. Establishing the necessary information systems for monitoring and allowing case managers the freedom to operate within agreed parameters are major and expensive challenges.

Contracts between local authorities and independent providers may give the former some influence over the terms of employment offered to their staff by the latter. Thus, some cost inflation may be welcome if it raises salaries and conditions of employment for traditionally poorly remunerated categories of staff or if it promotes equal opportunities. More likely, however, is that salary levels will be forced down in the more fiercely contested social care markets, since staff costs account for a high proportion of expenditure by most agencies.

There is also the simple problem of making like-with-like comparisons, for private and voluntary services may be cheaper by virtue of supporting less disabled, more independent users. Nevertheless, there is evidence that non-statutory services are more cost-effective than statutory when compared on a like-with-like basis (Knapp and Missiakoulis 1982; Judge and Knapp 1985; Knapp 1986; Beecham *et al.* 1991). Generally, however, the commonly-voiced assumption that markets for social care will introduce the kinds of competitive forces which push costs down is over-simplistic and perhaps over-optimistic. There might eventually be cost savings, but local authorities will need to ensure that the benefits accrue to them and not to the shareholders of private companies.

Quality

Suitably regulated contracts can enhance product quality and efficiency, but it is far easier to write quality clauses into some contracts than others, and most social care services do not lend themselves to unambiguous and readily monitored quality standards. There are reasons for not being too sanguine about the benefits of the new mixed economy for users and carers. Financial monitoring is considerably easier than quality assurance. Quality and outcome penalties of skimping on expenditure may not reveal themselves for some long time. Some groups of users may have difficulty expressing their views (in the absence of the necessary channels, or through disability unsupported by advocacy or communication aids). Moreover, the bureaucratization of provider agencies in response to the burdens of contracting may divert resources away from service delivery to administration.

On the other hand, the new arrangements for community care make it more likely that users will have a 'voice' in service selection and monitoring, enabling them to register their preferences and perspectives on outcomes in lieu of complex or expensive monitoring procedures. Nevertheless, a careful balance will need to be struck between the cost and inconvenience burdens (for all parties) of quality and outcome monitoring on the one hand, and the risk costs of occasional or superficial monitoring of inputs or basic service levels on the other hand. A second balance to be struck is between 'tight' and 'loose' specifications, the former possibly creating financial incentives for opportunistic suppliers to exploit loopholes, the latter perhaps leaving too much to chance or taking too much on trust.

Choice

Caring for People was confident in its assertion that 'stimulating the development of non-statutory service providers' will produce 'a wider range of choice of services', although the removal of the social security entitlement from many residents of private and voluntary residential and nursing homes has *narrowed* effective choice for this group. Rather a lot depends on whether authorities elect for block contracts with (virtual) monopoly providers. At the moment, a number of issues await resolution. What effective choices will be exercised by users or carers prior to referral or service placement, and how will they be constrained or stimulated by care managers? What range of choice will be offered to purchasers? At the area level, how far will choice of provision be circumscribed by service availability? Will the rerouting of social security funding for residential and nursing homes remove the choice which previously accompanied entitlement, or will it allow local authorities to promote a wider and more appropriate range of service options (especially non-residential services)? Will the Department of Health's directive on choice exert much of an influence, given its (selective) coverage of provider types but not service modes?

The inability or unwillingness of private and/or voluntary providers to enter a social care market, or to meet the standards laid down by local authorities, could limit the development of a broad choice range. The demise of smaller organizations in the face of high transaction costs could remove a distinctive dimension. However, the administrative attractions to the local authority of the block contract are equally threatening to the choice criterion. It should be remembered that governments often took responsibility for social care in the first place because they were not happy to leave the service to market forces, partly because some users of services were adjudged not to be able to bring sufficient consumer experience, competence or power to market negotiations. Because users may find it difficult to exercise informed choices, it falls to local authorities to regulate service quantity, characteristics and quality. But the process of regulation may encourage faithful adherence to those practices which are readily amenable to monitoring, to the neglect of other objectives or activities. It may also promote the standardization of product, *reducing* variety as private and voluntary providers are nudged closer to public sector requirements and characteristics (DiMaggio and Powell 1983). Innovation may be discouraged by regulators and may be financially inadvisable for non-statutory providers. Public authorities will need to work closely and supportively with independent providers to establish contractual links in such a way as not to threaten their diverse and important contributions. They should beware market fragmentation because of the excessive market power it could give some providers, while retaining an ability to respond to the diverse needs of individuals and populations.

Equity

Few local authority interviewees raised equity or fairness as an explicit concern, yet they were all committed to better targeting of services and resources on needs. In one form or another, equity must, and generally already does, underpin local authority allocations of funds and services. But, as Le Grand and others have pointed out, 'a common criticism of conventional markets (and a common justification for their replacement by bureaucracies) is that they foster and maintain inequalities and therefore social injustice' (Le Grand 1991: 1266).

A particular difficulty could arise, for example, if non-statutory providers are able to 'cream off' the less dependent and less costly clients, leaving the more costly residual for public sector providers. Market segmentation of this kind may be accompanied by market stratification by income or opportunity. Residualization of the poor may be the price of freedom of choice for the rich (Knapp 1989; Hoyes *et al.* 1991). On the other hand, the new mixed economy may offer previously untouched opportunities to disadvantaged groups of clients and their carers and, by searching out need and making explicit the criteria of allocation of resources, may achieve a better match between the two.

When considering the working of market forces, there is a sense in which social care is different. The nature of the product and the outcomes it is intended to achieve are themselves sources of distinctiveness and complication when compared with virtually every other local government service. Only in health care are outcomes almost as difficult to measure, but – in contrast to the health reforms which leave purchasing authorities largely operating in markets *internal* to the NHS – local authority social services departments are much more likely to be purchasing in '*external*' markets, with the voluntary and private sectors as major providers. NHS trusts working in the internal market have different aims and constraints from those of private, profit-seeking providers in the social care market. The purchaser/provider divide in the NHS separated two groups which were previously part of the same organization, and therefore were presumably sharing at least some of the same values, perspectives and directions. Independent social care providers, by contrast, might approach the new market from utterly different directions and with different prejudices from commissioners, bringing either the promise of innovation or the threat of conflict.

It is still possible to find some *laissez-faire* reformers 'wishing to administer a brisk restorative to the welfare state with a purging dose of market principles' (Taylor-Gooby and Lakeman 1988: 23) who set the weaknesses of the old community care system against the unattainable perfection of a perfectly functioning market complete with equality of opportunity or access. And there is no shortage of 'sentimental socialists' keen to ignore many of the inherent problems of a universalist system dominated by historical patterns of public sector provision when opposing the onward march of the market. Both groups will be trying to keep local authorities and markets as far as apart as possible, though for utterly different reasons.

The vast majority of the local authority officers and politicians interviewed hold views which are located some distance from the two ends of this spectrum. They express concerns about potential market failures which, combined with financial constraints and political caution (if not opposition), help to explain the widespread support for slow movement away from the steady state. Consequently, and as argued in this chapter, it is difficult to predict with confidence the form social care markets will take, or the extent to which they will promote the government's objectives of cost savings, quality, choice and equity.

Notes

1   By *socially efficient* we mean provision which minimizes the cost of achieving a given quality of service (or maximizes the user benefits or outcomes from a given cost), and which, via allocative efficiency, increases the range of choice. Efficiency will not necessarily produce an *equitable* allocation of resources, that is one which is fair by the criteria of social justice. In social care debates, social justice is usually defined by reference to judgements about individual needs.

2   This discussion, like the comments of our local authority interviewees and others, assumes that the public sector will remain the major purchaser of (formal) social care services for the foreseeable future. Were the public sector to shift substantially more of the burden of funding to service users or their relatives, we would need to address two further potential problems: *externalities* and the importance of *equity* objectives in social care. These issues were discussed at the level of principle in Knapp (1984: Chapter 6), and we consider some of the equity implications of the present reforms in the final section of this chapter. It is important to note, however, that user charges for public social care services remain a neglected research topic, yet are increasingly important sources of revenue to authorities, and it will probably not be long before privately funded long-term care insurance becomes a topic for much wider debate.

3   This embeddedness of the public and voluntary sectors places some limitations on the market behaviour of both (Seibel 1990). Whether or not it is for the good of either party will depend on individual circumstances, and it remains a question in need of empirical research.

4   These can only be considered briefly here. For more detail, see Kramer (1981, 1990), Knapp et al. (1990) and Gutch (1992).

5   Of course, the change from, on the one hand, a system of social security payments tied to individual residents and paid direct to homes to, on the other, contracts between local authorities and homes is a move from demand-side to supply-side subsidies, and one that *lessens*, but does not remove altogether, the distorting influences of third party payments.

6   Public works services, such as refuse collection and bus services, have tangible and easily specified outputs, and have no important distributional goals attached to them, and so are likely to be contracted out, and the contracts are likely to be let to the private sector. By contrast, control difficulties may leave governments more reluctant to contract out social care services, because of their obscure and complex outputs, and because redistribution is an important reason for intervention in the first place. Voluntary contractors are likely to be preferred to private for the same reasons. See Ferris and Graddy (1988, 1989) for an interesting test of these hypotheses with US data.

7

Residential care home transfers

Introduction

As indicated in Chapter 4, the decision to float off residential homes was generally prompted or considered by local authorities primarily on financial grounds. If the production of increased choice and other service improvements were not entirely ignored, the principal incentives were financial: first, the ability to access social security benefits (and therefore reduce revenue costs); and second, the ability to secure capital funds with which to upgrade other homes to registration standards.

As this kind of initiative was the most substantial development of a mixed economy of care, we undertook a more detailed study of this issue in a subsample of six of the twenty-four local authorities. This subsample was representative of the broad categories identified in the initial mapping: two of the six authorities which had already set up similar 'trusts' and were either certain or likely to transfer more services (referred to here as authorities A and B); two of the ten authorities which had decided definitely to float off some services but had not yet agreed the details, or which were likely to do so after taking legal and other advice (authorities C and D); and two of the five authorities which had ruled out transfer – one unconditionally (authority E) and one provisionally (authority F). In view of our guarantees of anonymity this chapter consists of a descriptive account across the six authorities. The aims of this study were:

- to describe authorities' rationales for transfer or retention of residential services;

- to describe possible legal, organizational, staffing and funding arrangements; and
- to identify any common issues and problems.

It is worth noting at the outset one problem encountered in negotiating access, which indicates the changing cultural climate referred to elsewhere in this book. In the case of authority C, the council's response to our request for the sort of information made available by other authorities was, first, that this information was subject 'to confidentiality obligations' between itself and the company established to manage its transferred homes and, second, that details of the transfer were to be 'incorporated into a package of documents for sale to other local authorities'. The information could be purchased, subject to agreement on how it would be used. It was made clear that having itself purchased the information at considerable expense from management consultants and leading counsel, the authority was unwilling to share it freely with academic researchers. This stance, it was said, was both reasonable and a pointed illustration of the commercial ethos that authorities had been urged to embrace in creating a mixed economy of care.

The national legislative and policy context

This section describes the policy context, from *Caring for People* onwards, within which local authorities considered residential home transfers. In effect, authorities were responding to a window of opportunity – in terms of financial incentives – which was gradually closed, but not completely shut, by the government. A brief chronology of the main policy pronouncements is given in Box 7.1. Our intention was thus to chart developments in relation to perceived changes in incentives and disincentives throughout three periods of time: prior to the Audit Commission's draft circular in November 1990; between this date and the publication of the government's guidance in August 1991; and after this guidance was issued.

Caring for People foresaw social services departments not only making use 'wherever possible' of services from voluntary, not-for-profit and private providers but also, in their absence, actively stimulating the creation of such agencies (Secretaries of State 1989b: paras 3.4.1 and 3.4.5). Local authorities could promote the mixed economy by, *inter alia*, 'taking steps to stimulate the setting up of 'not-for-profit' agencies' and 'identifying areas of their own work...sufficiently self-contained to be suitable for 'floating off' as self-managing units' (*ibid.*: para. 3.4.6).

The sixth of the White Paper's key objectives was to secure 'better value for taxpayers' money by introducing a new funding structure for social care', with the aim 'that social security provisions should not, as they do now, provide any incentive in favour of residential and nursing home care' (*ibid.*: para. 1.16). To end this perverse incentive, the government proposed to introduce a new funding structure

---

Box 7.1   Brief chronology of policy pronouncements

November 1989, Caring for People: local authorities to diversify provision, *inter alia*, by 'floating off' areas of their own work. Proposed funding changes create financial incentives to transfer local authority residential homes to the independent sector.

November 1990, Audit Commission draft circular. Questions the independence – and therefore the legality – of the proposed not-for-profit trusts being proposed and established for some local authorities' transfers.

January 1991, ministerial promise of guidance: Mrs Bottomley announces that the Department of Health will provide guidance to local authorities setting out the government's attitude to such transfers. Aim to be produced by April 1991.

August 1991, Department of Health guidance issued (LAC(91)12): Residents of such transferred homes would remain the responsibility of the local authority – for which, thereby, the financial incentives were significantly reduced.

---

for those seeking public support for residential and nursing homes as from April 1991...After that date local authorities will take responsibility for financial support for people in private and voluntary homes over and above any general social security entitlements. The new arrangements will not, however, apply to people already resident in homes before April 1991. (*ibid.*: para. 1.12)

The consequence of the latter group of residents having 'preserved rights' was, in effect, to present local authorities with a 'window of opportunity'. Authorities able to transfer homes before 1 April 1991 would gain 'protected status' for all transferred residents and thus make revenue savings equivalent to the benefits they received. In practice, few of the twenty-four sample authorities were in a position, in late 1990 and early 1991, to take advantage of this 'window of opportunity'. By contrast, other authorities – for example, Somerset, Dorset and the Isle of Wight – within weeks of the White Paper's publication had devised plans for transferring homes before 31 March 1991.

For its part the government wanted 'to ensure that local authorities have every incentive to make use of the independent sector when placing people in residential settings' (*ibid.*: para. 3.7.10). All authorities would 'need to review the extent to which they need to maintain homes of their own [and] some rationalization is likely to be required' (*ibid.*: para. 3.7.11). Moreover, the new social security arrangements contained incentives for them to do so. The government's original intention was to transfer the funds provided to residents in residential care and nursing homes from the Department of Social Security (DSS) benefit vote to the Personal Social Services Standard Spending Assessment (SSA) over a number of years. As a result of the decision on 18 July 1990 to phase in the community care changes, these funding changes were to take place over the three financial years 1993/94 to 1995/96. However, the consequence of this delay was that the 'window of opportunity' for home transfers was kept for a further two years.

This then was the context in late 1990, with authorities being urged: first, to consider residential care as only a last resort; second, to use the independent residential sector whenever possible; and third, to review – with a view to reducing in number – their own homes. As an 'incentive', they would be responsible in full, from 1 April 1993, for the costs of residents in local authority homes, whereas residents in non-local authority homes before that date would have their benefit entitlements preserved. To local authorities there appeared, therefore, to be a clear financial incentive to increase the number of residents with protected status prior to 1 April 1993, and thus to transfer local authority homes to the independent sector.

The rationale for transferring or retaining homes can, however, be considered at three different levels: first, at the level of general principle; second, in terms of proportions for retention or transfer; and third, the criteria for determining which individual homes to retain or transfer.

General arguments for and against transfers

Two of the six authorities were identified in our initial mapping as having considered but rejected home transfers, one unconditionally and one provisionally (authorities E and F respectively). In authority E this outright rejection was primarily political and based on the strongly held belief among members of the ruling group 'that the best services are those provided directly by the local authority'. Thus there was hostility to putting viable homes into any other form of ownership. Although internal reports had identified substantial revenue savings to be gained from a transfer programme, the members considered that any transfer would undermine binding no-redundancy agreements with the trades unions. This authority opted instead to close the homes in the poorest physical condition – with the highest upgrading costs – and redeploy the staff in order to improve staffing ratios in the remaining local authority homes (including two that were newly built). In rejecting transfers, members were also reflecting a strong pride in local authority provision and what one member described as 'a reasonable suspicion of the mixed economy'.

Authority F had provisionally rejected home transfers because of uncertainties about their legal status and the financial benefits to be obtained. In terms of a broad rationale this authority can be considered with the other four, for each of which the rationale for transfer comprised a composite of the following:

- broad policy aims, in terms of decreasing public provision and encouraging alternative providers within a mixed economy of care;
- specific service principles, in respect of user choice and improving care standards;
- fulfilling statutory responsibilities;
- meeting service needs by matching provision with assessed degrees of dependence, demographic trends and forecasts of future need; and
- taking advantage of both capital and revenue financial incentives.

Prior to November 1990, for three of these five authorities (C, D and F) the principal, but not the sole, reason for considering home transfers undoubtedly was the last.

The need for a broad shift from residential to non-residential care had been accepted by all six authorities before the 1990 NHS and Community Care Act (even by authority E) and in most cases such developments had been in train for some years. Prior to the government's decision on phased implementation in July 1990, the intention of authority A had been to continue funding this shift from the transferred social security budget. When this funding transfer was delayed for two years, officers began investigating other ways 'to transfer funding from residential homes towards community care'. Members were advised in November 1990 that to achieve this transition 'it would be necessary to place the management of some residential care in the hands of an organization that is separate from the local authority'. Both officers and members were adamant that this proposal was not 'finance-led' but based on long-term service advantages; that is, on extending the range of supply and providing wider choice. However, the enforced delay meant that the authority considered that it was bound to take advantage of the financial incentives created.

In authority B, by contrast, consideration of home transfers was, according to the Director, 'purely for budgetary reasons...because of the incentives that have been set up that way'. Echoing this view, the social services committee Chair argued that the proposal did not have 'much to say for it professionally or politically: it's not actually going to produce anything better...it is definitely a finance-led move because we think it would save us money and it may generate a bit of money.' In addition, the members' view was that 'we don't want to part company with anything that we don't have to unless we feel that there's actually something in it for users'. Furthermore, the Labour administration had spent 'a huge amount of money' since the mid-1980s upgrading its homes. Unlike the other five authorities, it did not now need to spend large capital sums to bring its own homes up to the Registered Homes Act 1984 standards. More than that, however, like authority E which rejected home transfers unconditionally, it took considerable pride in its homes. The consideration of transfers was, therefore, driven by the need to make revenue savings – in the context of severe, authority-wide, financial pressures – and the availability of funding which appeared to offer such savings.

For each of the other authorities, bringing their own homes up to registration standards would be extremely expensive. In addition, the necessary capital improvements had to be made quickly and would inevitably lead to a reduction in available places, as shared rooms were replaced by single ones. The sums involved in this upgrading were, it was said, far beyond the scope of authorities' limited capital expenditure programmes. Although none of the other three authorities proposing home transfers (C, D and F) couched its arguments in such straightforwardly financial terms – each maintaining that the promotion of alternative suppliers, and the attendant increase in user choice, were just as important – they all acknowledged that the twin pressures of the available financial incentives (both capital and revenue) and the disincentives were crucial to their consideration of transfers.

One important factor to consider for authorities proposing transfers was the proportion of homes to be retained as local authority homes. There were four factors which led authorities to reject wholesale transfers:

- the need to fulfil their statutory duties;
- the need to ensure flexibility and choice in a mixed economy of care;
- the need to provide a benchmark both for service standards and for costs elsewhere; and
- the need to ensure against market failure.

Caring for People expressed the expectation that local authorities would retain the ability to act as direct service providers if other forms of service provision were unforthcoming or unsuitable (para. 4.11). This was a general expectation about all services and did not represent any specific reminder about statutory duties. However, according to Circular LAC(91)12, 'Section 42 of the NHS and Community Care Act, which is to be implemented in April 1993, will require authorities to make some direct provision for residential care under Section 21 of the 1948 Act' (Department of Health 1991c: para. 5). Under this latter legislation, local authorities have an enabling duty to arrange for the provision – but not necessarily themselves wholly to provide – residential accommodation for people in need. What was not clear from Circular LAC(91)12 was the meaning of 'some': what constituted an appropriate proportion for retention?

Authority A regarded one-third to be an appropriate proportion of all homes to be transferred. In proposing to retain control of the remainder, the authority took what was described as 'a clear decision' to retain 'the ability to act as a direct service provider'. Authority D considered options which involved transferring between 50 and 80 per cent of its homes. The latter figure was explicitly rejected on the Director's advice that retaining only 20 per cent of homes 'would fail to satisfy the legal requirements placed on the

Committee by the National Assistance Act 1948 and would not offer a reasonable degree of choice to people needing residential care'. In this case the authority decided to transfer 50 per cent of its homes.

The other two authorities considering transfer (B and C) decided to retain in local authority control 12 and 50 per cent of their places respectively. All authorities considered it imperative to retain a sufficient number of local authority homes to provide a safeguard in the event of the failure of non-statutory providers. (The legal aspects of this issue are discussed further on pages 124–7.)

It was also commonly argued that local authorities should retain some of their own homes to act as a benchmark – a 'measure of excellence' – for other providers: not only in terms of standards of care and staffing levels, but also in terms of costs. As one social services interviewee remarked, after 1993 there was the potential for 'major conflict' when social services departments would be able to say 'we know what our unit costs are, we know what our staffing levels are; why should the private homes down the road charge £100 a week more?'

The principal criteria for retaining individual homes were their physical condition and physical location. Thus, in shire counties, for example, authorities wished to retain an adequate geographical coverage of homes. In all cases authorities sought to retain those homes in the best physical condition and best able to be developed as resource centres providing a range of care services.

Revenue incentives for transfers

Before November 1990: opening the 'window of opportunity'

Given the extent of the resource pressures and constraints under which they regarded themselves as operating, it is unsurprising that authorities should have sought to maximize the revenue incentives (and minimize the disincentives) perceived to be associated with home transfers: both before and after the transfer of social security funds on 1 April 1993 there was a disincentive to manage residential homes directly, and a corresponding incentive to transfer them to the independent sector.

When the six authorities were first considering home transfers in late 1990 and early 1991, they could readily calculate the likely revenue benefits. After 1 April 1993 people newly entering voluntary and private homes would be entitled to claim income support at what was then the basic weekly level (£37.50, or £54.50 for people with disabilities) and housing benefit (then approximately £25 per week). By contrast, people newly entering local authority homes after 1 April 1993 would not be entitled to housing benefit. (In March 1992 the latter was replaced by a residential allowance: throughout this chapter, which deals with authorities' considerations prior to this date, we refer to housing benefit.) This entitlement was one 'clear benefit incentive' in favour of independent homes after 1 April 1993, but it was a relatively minor incentive compared to that which existed in respect of people already resident in private and voluntary homes on 1 April 1993. Here the benefit entitlements (in late 1990 and early 1991) ranged from £155 to £230 per week depending on the individual's degree of dependency and the home's location (see Table 7.1). This compared with the entitlement of existing residents in local authority homes to the special rate of income support – the residential accommodation rate – which in 1990/91 was £46.90.

Prior to 1 April 1993, new residents in transferred homes (but not in local authority homes) would become eligible for higher benefits, subject to Department of Social Security adjudication officers' decisions about the independence of homes from local authority control (see the next section). Moreover, these benefits would be protected thereafter. After 1 April 1993, even though the scale of the difference would decrease (as the numbers of residents with protected status fell) residents in private and voluntary homes would still have the advantage of eligibility for housing benefit denied to residents in local authority homes. In other words, since the benefit rights of existing residents in private and voluntary homes on 1 April 1993 were protected, there was a clear incentive for local authorities to transfer homes prior to that date, thereby enabling residents to claim higher benefits not only from the time of transfer but after 1 April 1993 until their deaths. Here was the 'window of opportunity', clear and open, pre-November 1990.

Thus, although none of the six authorities had moved with the speed of some authorities elsewhere, they would still secure appreciable advantages if they could effect transfers before April 1993; although for an increasingly shorter period as 1 April 1993 approached. Moreover, as we examine in the following section, while the same revenue incentives and disincentives effectively remained intact until August 1991, it became increasingly unclear whether the benefits would indeed accrue.

November 1990 to August 1991: uncertainty and 'planning blight'

The immediate problem for authorities considering taking advantage of this 'window of opportunity' – apart from any fundamental political opposition – was ensuring that any transfer did enable residents to claim the higher benefits. Only by so doing would authorities make the anticipated revenue savings. There were two aspects to this problem. First, social security payments are individual entitlements and cannot be claimed by either social services departments or other home proprietors. The precise financial outcome of any transfer is therefore unknown until individual residents' claims have been dealt with by the DSS. Second, the benefit regulations are subject to independent interpretations by local DSS adjudication officers: moreover, these officers make decisions about eligibility – and judgements about a project's independence – only after projects are in operation. Thus, although authorities could

Table 7.1 Income support: residential care homes, 1990–1992 (£ per week)

	April 1990		August 1990		April 1991		April 1992	
	Within London	Outside London	Within London	Outside London	Within London	Outside London	Within London	Outside London
Elderly	173	150	178	155	183	160	200	175
Very dependent or blind elderly	188	165	193	170	208	185	230	205
Mentally ill	173	150	178	155	193	170	210	185
Suffering from drug or alcohol dependency	173	150	178	155	193	170	210	185
Mentally handicapped	198	175	203	180	218	195	240	215
Physically disabled and disablement begun under pension age	233	210	238	215	253	230	270	245
Other (including physically disabled over pension age)	173	150	178	155	183	160	200	175
Personal expenses	10.55	10.55	10.55	10.55	11.40	11.40	n.a.	n.a.

Source: House of Commons Social Security Committee (1991: Appendix, p. xxix).

be fairly certain of the general criteria by which transfers would be judged – genuine independence from local authority control and genuine choice of home for existing residents – they were unsure how any particular scheme would be judged.

Before November 1990, three of the six authorities (A, C and D) were confident that they would be able to meet the criteria and saw the need to effect transfers as rapidly as possible. As one Director said in October 1990: 'if the Committee agrees to move swiftly we are optimistic that it will be possible for a new independent body to secure for its residents the higher level benefits currently available to people in independent care not only until 31 March 1993 but also beyond that date.' This optimism was dented somewhat the following month by the Audit Commission's draft circular, which questioned not just the prudence but also the legality of transferring homes out of local authority control to not-for-profit trusts. This circular caused, in the first place, general concern that the Commission had overstepped its brief by formulating a legal position, and second, particular concern that by questioning the independence and legality of the proposed not-for-profit organizations the Commission was undermining their whole viability. If they were deemed not to be independent of local authorities they would not attract higher social security benefits and a large part of the financial rationale for their establishment would disappear. As the Director of one of the six authorities remarked, it 'had the apparent intention of blocking all management transfers other than by the sale of empty houses'.

Among other things, such uncertainty provided a great deal of work for the barristers whose opinions about the legality of proposals individual authorities sought. The authorities in this study voiced considerable irritation about the costs of this advice, costs which they could ill afford at a time of severe financial constraints (and in some cases actual service cuts), and, more importantly, costs which would have been unnecessary if there had been clear guidance from the Department of Health after the Audit Commission's intervention. Acknowledging the need for clarity, in January 1991 the Minister of Health promised government guidance. In the event, as we have noted, it was not published until August 1991, despite having been promised for April.

It is possible at this stage to divide the six authorities into two groups, only one of which – comprising authorities A, C and D – had hired management consultants to advise on the options and procedures for transfer. This considerable investment was, in itself, a measure of their commitment to evaluating the advantages and disadvantages of home transfers, in whatever form. It also enabled all three authorities to access experience being accumulated by their consultants from similar work in other local authorities. By contrast, the three authorities that did not engage management consultants had no such pool of experience and legal opinion to draw on. In two cases (B and F), therefore, the Audit Commission's intervention added considerably to their doubts about the wisdom of proceeding with any exploration of home transfers. (The third – authority E – was opposed to any kind of transfer.)

Thus, in January 1991, the social services committee in authority F was advised by its officers that, while some benefits of independent management could be identified, 'the legal position is unclear, and uncertainties about the potential financial benefits to local authorities are emerging'. Given the nature and extent of these uncertainties – including the authority solicitor's doubt about local authorities' powers to establish not-for-profit companies to manage residential homes – the authority decided to make no decision pending the 'forthcoming advice from the Department of Health, the Department of Social Security and the Audit Commission'. In practice, too, it was acknowledged that the authority was happy to put the issue 'on the back burner' because there was neither the management capacity to appraise the issues fully nor the political will to do so.

In authority B, officers reported to the social services committee in early April 1991 that an opportunity for financial savings still existed and that such savings would last from 1991 until approximately 1995, 'by which time the effect of the phased transfer of funds from social security to the local authority would have cancelled out any savings'. The Director of Social Services described the financial incentives as 'a deliberate mechanism designed to achieve the mixed economy of care' and advised members to be cautious about the financial gains possible. First, there was the risk that the DSS would judge transferred homes as not properly independent of the local authority, with the consequence that residents could be ineligible for higher social security benefits. Second, this was 'a highly complex area...subject to conflict and fast-changing advice from government departments'. Counsel's opinion on any proposed transfer would be essential, but the experience of authorities elsewhere, even where this had been obtained, suggested a national picture of continuing great uncertainty with some authorities succeeding and others failing to obtain enhanced benefits for transferred residents. The position was described as one of 'planning blight', pending the Department of Health's guidance in April. The committee decided to await this 'definitive advice' and assess the financial benefits later that month before considering further any transfer. The Director's view was that the latter would have to be substantial to persuade his members to agree to any transfer.

Although the authority continued to consider the matter, it decided in August 1991 that Circular LAC(91)12 so eroded the financial incentives as to make home transfers not viable. This authority was the only one of the six for which access to capital for upgrading was not an important consideration. Once the incentive of revenue gains had been removed, the advantages of transfer were regarded as having disappeared and no further moves were taken towards transfers.

After August 1991: closing the 'window of opportunity'

In simultaneous written parliamentary answers on 25 June, the Secretaries of State for Social Security and Health spelt out the government's position; this was then amplified in Circular LAC(91)12, which, in draft, was subject to a brief period of consultation. In essence there were three main points. First, the government confirmed its commitment to the development by local authorities of a mixed economy of care. Second, it reiterated the need for local authorities to consider reducing their direct provision of residential homes and, where appropriate, transferring their management to the independent sector. Third, it proposed to treat residents of transferred homes as remaining the responsibility of the local authority concerned; and as residents in local authority accommodation they would not, therefore, be eligible for any higher rates of benefit. When Circular LAC(91)12 took effect on 12 August 1991, the window of opportunity was closed, but not completely shut: the revenue incentive for transfer was reduced to the amount available via housing benefit.

Revenue benefits were, however, only part of the perceived financial advantage to authorities in transferring homes. Consequently, Circular LAC-(91)12 did not affect three of the authorities proposing transfers (A, C and D), in none of which were revenue savings the principal rationale. For example, in authority D the circular merely confirmed expectations that the most optimistic of its assumptions about benefit entitlements were unrealistic. Its principal interest, however, was access to capital for upgrading homes; therefore, although there would 'not be any financial saving', the Director's advice to members was that the proposed transfer still represented 'the cheapest and most practical way of funding the conversion work which is required, unless members wish to pursue other options such as closing homes'.

Legal and organizational issues associated with transfer

One of the first questions facing local authorities considering homes transfers was their legality. As one authority's leading legal adviser remarked, 'It has been a tortuous process for local authorities to interpret the Department of Health's requirements. There has been an absence of positive direction and guidance.' The transfer process was characterized by legal complexities and uncertainties in the areas of land and property, personnel and organizational form. This uncertainty led the Association of Directors of Social Services in July 1991 to respond to the Department of Health's draft circular (subsequently LAC(91)12) by voicing their

> disappointment that instead of supplying a clear lead in these respects, the Department has, instead, exhorted social services authorities to consult their own legal advisers on some contentious issues. It has been hoped that the Department's own advice would have rendered that unnecessary, instead of making it almost obligatory. (Association of Directors of Social Services 1991)

The Association illustrated its members' 'general dismay' by quoting one Director's view that the circular 'will not help authorities find a way through the legal complexities. We should urge the Department of Health to be more specific in its guidance.' The circular led the Director in one of the six authorities to remark that it 'leaves the legality of any proposed management transfer open to divergent interpretations'.

Two of the most important considerations for authorities were: first (as discussed in the preceding section), that they were meeting their statutory duties under the terms of the National Assistance Act 1948; and second, that the proposed organization was not a 'controlled' (or 'arm's-length') or 'influenced' company under the terms of the Local Government and Housing Act 1989.

As regards the former, the legal advice given to the local authorities in this study was that they must retain direct control of a proportion of their homes. There are examples outside the study of authorities, notably Somerset, which transferred all their homes; but the advice given to the local authorities in this subsample – by their own solicitors, externally appointed management consultants and leading counsel – was that they risked being in default of their responsibilities under the 1948 Act unless they retained some homes. Authorities were also advised of the need to demonstrate that any transfer was set in the context of a strategy for improving services and not pursued solely for financial gain. Equally, for audit purposes they needed to be able to demonstrate that they were not incurring any financial loss or, indeed, more broadly incurring any undue financial risk.

As regards the 1989 Local Government and Housing Act, its principal requirement was that authorities could demonstrate the independence of the new body from the authority itself: that is, that it was a 'minority interest' organization with local authority representation no higher than 19 per cent. Local authorities can, however, exercise significant 'control' over new organizations in other ways: first, through their role as registration authority; second, as prime contractors for places; and third, through restrictive covenants on leases.

The question of independence was, as indicated previously, also crucial to the issue of transferred residents' eligibility for social security benefits. DSS adjudication officers would make their decision in the light of whether the new organization was genuinely independent of the council and whether residents had been able to choose whether they wanted a place in the transferred home. This remained the case after LAC(91)12, but new residents in transferred homes were eligible for higher benefits only if these criteria of independence were met.

Organizational forms

Organizational options broadly comprised a trust, a company limited by guarantee, a housing association, a management buy-out and an employee share ownership scheme. In each case, authorities could use either an existing or a new organization.

As indicated in Chapter 4, the last two options were seriously considered by few of the twenty-four sample authorities. They were not treated as realistic options by any of the six authorities in this study. The trust option was considered by three of the four authorities which formulated transfer proposals but was rejected, largely on management consultants' advice about the personal liability of trustees for contracts entered into and because of the legal complexity of establishing such trusts. Only in authority B was transfer to a housing association the preferred option. In authorities A, C and D the option of a company limited by guarantee was preferred for three reasons: the relative speed and simplicity of its establishment; flexibility in terms of any subsequent changes to aims and objectives; and the limited liability of individual directors. It was also generally acknowledged that this organizational form was the one most readily comprehensible to those lending institutions from which the companies would be seeking capital for upgrading.

In parenthesis, it is worth noting that there has been some confusion about nomenclature in this area: the limited company established in one authority in 1990 is in fact called a housing trust and is controlled by a Board of Trustees who, in company law, comprise its directors. Local authority representation on the board is less than 20 per cent of the total, thereby rendering the organization neither a controlled nor an influenced company within the meaning of the 1989 Local Government and Housing Act. The same condition applied to the new limited companies proposed in the other two authorities. In each of these three cases, other board directors were selected to represent a range of general management expertise in the provision of community care services in general and housing management in particular. In none of the three cases did the authority advertise nationally for bids from existing organizations to take over managing their services.

Organizational process

In Chapter 4, we raised the question of how far authorities' development of a mixed economy of care was a corporate rather than a departmental initiative. We noted the variability across the twenty-four authorities and the limited extent to which this was a genuinely corporate concern. Residential home transfers were, however, a matter of serious authority-wide concern in the six authorities in this study. In part, this concern reflected the pre-eminently political nature of home transfers, but it transcended social services department boundaries for other reasons too.

First, in a legal sense the transfer of residential homes cannot be anything other than an issue of corporate concern. As one local authority Secretary reminded members of the social services committee, their prime task was to satisfy themselves 'on policy and service delivery issues', but in reaching a decision they were 'required to consider whether a transfer represented the best use of financial resources'. If the committee could not demonstrate the latter, it laid itself open to challenge from external auditors. In each of the six authorities, consideration of strategic principles involved senior members from across the council; and in each case where transfers were proposed the issues of operational implementation involved officers from a range of departments, notably chief executive's, finance, solicitors, land and property, and personnel.

A crucial part of the process of considering transfer proposals was the consultation with all parties involved: residents, their families and carers, staff and trades unions. In each of the three authorities concerned the consultation exercises were exhaustive, not just to allay the concerns of residents and staff but also to meet the requirement that residents had exercised an informed choice and that staff had been fully appraised of potential changes to their terms and conditions of service.

Staffing issues associated with transfer

As noted in Chapter 4, the main consideration about establishing not-for-profit organizations was that they should be sufficiently independent of the local authority for residents to be eligible for social security benefits, but sufficiently linked to it that it would retain some control over such key issues as staffing and quality of care. The former was a major area of concern because:

- it was a central tenet that transfers should not be to the detriment of existing residents or staff;
- authorities' commitments to residents and their families that there would be the least possible disruption in any transfer raised the possibility of staff retention in order to preserve existing resident–staff relationships;
- some authorities had firm no-redundancy agreements with their staff groups and unions;
- other authorities wished to minimize redundancies both as 'good employers' and as a means of avoiding large redundancy payments.

At first sight, the authorities considering not-for-profit organizations had two broad options: to second or to transfer staff to the new organization. In practice, the first option was ruled out by legal advice that secondment would prejudice the essential rule of independence, and therefore residents would be ineligible for social security benefits. This advice was based in part upon the experience of authorities outside the subsample: for example, of South Glamorgan, whose transfer proposal became the subject of a judicial review instituted by the Audit Commission. The option of staff transfer, however, raised important and complex issues in employment law, most notably in respect of the Employment Protection (Consolidation) Act 1978 and the Transfer of Undertakings (Protection of Employment) Regulations 1981. Before looking at the implications of this legislation, it is important to bear in mind the two main staffing considerations of the authorities considering homes transfers: first, they were seeking to obtain for staff a transfer which would preserve their jobs and preserve or enhance their terms and conditions of service; and second, they wished to avoid redundancy payments, either from staff who could not or would not accept the transfer, or from staff who transferred but claimed redundancy in the process.

One of the first considerations under the legislation is whether the transfer of local authority residential homes to a not-for-profit company constitutes a commercial venture: if it does not, then the 1981 Regulations do not apply. The balance of legal advice to the local authorities in this study was that home transfers to not-for-profit companies would be outside the scope of these Regulations because, by definition, they were to be run as non-profit-making, rather than 'commercial', ventures. This would not be the case if the local authority was proposing transfers to profit-making private contractors.

It is important to stress, however, that although this was the balance of legal opinion, there were some important caveats about the consistency of the Regulations with European Community directives and the possibility of industrial tribunals taking a contrary view of the transfers not comprising commercial undertakings. The implication of this contrary view was that staff would first have to be made redundant by the local authority and then re-employed by the new companies: the local authorities would risk liability to redundancy payments for effectively unfair dismissal.

The latter raises the possibility of a further complication for local authorities – one which did arise for one of the authorities in this study, where the balance of legal opinion was that the proposed transfer would not fall within the remit of the 1981 Regulations but would instead be covered by Section 94 of the Employment Protection (Consolidation) Act 1978. However, it was a view not wholly shared by the legal adviser to the authority's external auditors; on which basis the latter said that the authority's members 'should be advised that there is a degree of uncertainty in this area relating to the application of the law. The financial risks attaching to any decision they take if subsequently a challenge is made should be explained and evaluated.' The authority's own senior legal adviser duly reported to members that although not in accordance with the auditor's solicitor his advice was unchanged.

On the basis that homes transferred to a not-for-profit company did not fall within the remit of the 1981 Regulations, the authorities proposing transfer have done so under the terms of the 1978 Employment Protection (Consolidation) Act. Here the key part of the legislation is Section 94, which deals with employees' rights upon the change of ownership of a business. In certain circumstances, staff with two or more years' service (part-time or full-time) would be entitled to claim redundancy payments. However, under the terms of Section 94 such claims can be resisted if two conditions are met: first, that the new employer (the new not-for-profit company) offers the local authority staff suitable employment before ending their employment with the local authority; second, 'suitable' means that employees moving to the new company should do so on terms and conditions of service which preserve or enhance their existing rights, in respect, for example, of pensions, holiday entitlement and sick pay. Where the new terms or conditions differ they should relate to alternative work which, again, is 'reasonable': which, for example, do not include substantial changes in working hours or shifts.

After transfer, staff have a four-week trial period and can resign and claim constructive dismissal if they think their new terms and conditions are unsuitable and to their detriment. Such claims would be judged on the criteria of reasonableness – the reasonableness of the new job *vis-à-vis* the previous job and the reasonableness of the employee in rejecting the new job. This same criterion of reasonableness applies when staff decide to decline the transfer on the basis of the original offer: they can claim redundancy from the local authority only if they can demonstrate – to an industrial tribunal – that they have acted reasonably in refusing the offer. It is also worth noting that tribunals make such judgements on the basis of their assessment of the facts in individual cases and not on the basis of any clear legal definition.

In the cases in this study, the clear intention of the local authorities concerned, and that of the not-for-profit companies they established, was to secure for their staff a transfer which was reasonable in terms of preserving, or enhancing, terms and conditions of service. Despite this explicit broad aim to act reasonably and to provide staff with suitable new employment, a number of concerns clearly remained. First, from the point of view of staff and unions, there is the question of how binding are agreements with the new companies; by definition they will be outside local authorities' direct control, if not their influence. Further, the new companies, encouraged by the authorities, would inevitably seek to alter some working practices. Could local authorities guarantee that after six, twelve or eighteen months the new companies would not amend terms and conditions of service to the perceived detriment of staff? By this stage, the terms of the 1978 Act would be inapplicable, the original reasonableness of the employer (in offering essentially unaltered terms and conditions) having been sufficient to forestall redundancy claims. It would appear to follow that perhaps the most prudent course for local authorities in any transfer would be to persuade the new company to re-employ staff on exactly the same terms and conditions and to 'conceal' any intention to alter terms and conditions of service materially in the future. But even in these cases, staff would be entitled to decline the transfer and claim redundancy if, for example, they could show that the move was unreasonable by virtue of the new company's unproven competence as an employer.

In practice, the charge of unreasonableness may have been a difficult one to sustain in the cases of the companies established or proposed by the authorities in this study. In the case of one, for example, the new company improved rates of pay and preserved other staff terms and conditions, including trade union recognition, equal opportunities, health and safety policies and grievance procedures. Moreover, each of the three local authorities concerned was careful to ensure the fullest possible consultation with all affected staff and trade unions.

One general point to emerge from this consideration of staffing issues surrounding transfers was that, in the view of some of those involved, the legal complexities, uncertainties and costs may in themselves be sufficient to deter other authorities from investigating the possibility of such transfers.

Land and property issues associated with transfer

Essentially, authorities proposing to transfer homes have three options: freehold sale, leasehold sale and leasehold transfer (that is, rental).

The disposal of local authority assets is constrained by the requirements of Section 123 of the Local Government Act 1972; in particular by subsection 2 under which local authorities cannot dispose of assets – except on a short tenancy, of less than seven years – 'for a consideration less than can reasonably be obtained' without the express consent of the Secretary of State for the Environment. This 'best consideration' clause is normally taken to equal open market value. In other words, they cannot transfer assets – even to a not-for-profit organization – on a preferential basis without the Secretary of State's permission: that is, they cannot undervalue assets to secure a transfer.

However, what constitutes 'best consideration' is far from straightforward. For example, authorities could transfer leaseholds with restrictive covenants which would substantially affect, and reduce, their market value. The latter, indeed, was what authorities in this study did to ensure that the transferred homes would remain in use as residential care homes. Such covenants affect the market value by restricting what would otherwise be the potential development value of the assets: that is, their market value calculated on the basis of some alternative use. In this case, the authorities were advised, 'best consideration' could be defined not as some 'nominal' highest price, but in terms of the councils' broad service policy objectives.

It is an indication of the problems facing local authorities in this situation that one authority proposed a leasehold sale on the above covenanted basis and was advised not only by its own legal officers but informally by the Department of the Environment that 'best consideration' was rightly judged on the basis of the use to which the transferred properties would be put, subject to the conditions of the lease. The legal adviser to the authority's external auditors, however, took a different view. The auditors therefore suggested that the authority: first, seek 'formal confirmation' from the Department of the Environment that the Secretary of State's consent was not required; and second, establish the open market values of individual properties, on the basis of potential development values. This suggestion was dismissed as inappropriate, not least because under the terms of the covenants in question the local authority in effect retained any alternative development values by disallowing changes of use.

Once authorities had satisfied themselves that the 'disposal' in question did not require the Secretary of State's consent, they faced the question of the precise nature of the transfer – by freehold sale, by leasehold sale (with capital premiums) or by leasehold transfer. The first option was not taken up by any of the authorities within the study. It was rejected partly because the local authorities wished to retain, long-term, their property holdings and partly because such disposal would make it more difficult to include enforceable restrictive covenants. Although generally acknowledged to be the most administratively convenient option, and the one likely to produce the largest, most immediate, capital receipts, it was firmly rejected on the grounds of both short-term and long-term security. The latter was security in terms of authorities' future ability to respond to 'market failures'; the former was concerned with the adverse effect that proposed sales would have on residents, families and staff. The second option of leasehold sale was also in each case eventually rejected because of the need to enhance the new companies' ability to obtain finance from lending institutions: an ability, authorities were advised, which would be impaired if they had to pay large capital premiums at the outset. It is the latter, payable on transfer, which would have provided local authorities with immediate capital receipts; receipts which one authority in particular was proposing to use to finance the upgrading of other homes and which thereby represented one of the main incentives for transfer.

In practice, as the negotiations in this authority were concluded it was accepted – as it was by the other two authorities in this study – that the new company could not be burdened with a large initial capital premium. The alternative was for a leasehold transfer with annual rental payments: payments equivalent over time to this capital sum. Once paid the rental would be on a peppercorn basis of, for example, £1 per annum.

Summary and conclusions

The transfer of local authority homes to the independent sector was the main area of development identified in the initial phase of the study: it was where the incentives and disincentives – especially the revenue incentives – were perceived to be the most apparent and most immediate. In October 1992 three of the six authorities had successfully concluded transfer arrangements, each to not-for-profit limited companies. Of the other three authorities, one was opposed on principle to transfers and another concluded that after Circular LAC(91)12 the revenue incentives had virtually disappeared. The remaining authority was seeking to resolve its revenue problems by selling home places to the NHS: this approach, the Director said, not only yielded 'quite a lot of revenue to actually improve the quality of care' but was 'more advantageous than fiddling about with income support'.

While it is important to stress that financial gain was not the sole rationale for transfer, it is equally important to emphasize the financial context within which transfers were being considered. Thus, according to each of the authorities involved, revenue savings accruing from transfer were a vital concern for social services committees charged (at the time of our fieldwork) with making significant revenue savings across a range of existing services.

In the case of one authority, for example, none of the costed options presented by management consultants in April 1991 was judged to 'achieve the level of savings required in 1991/92', even though each option would produce long-term savings significant enough to allow the authority 'to redirect resources...to new community care initiatives'. The Director of Social Services reminded the committee that the transfer proposal had been produced 'in the context of both the NHS and Community Care Act 1990 and the financial constraints faced by the Council'. The social services department was, he said, 'considerably constrained' in its budget for the coming year, in which pro-visional savings of £300,000 had been identified from home transfers. If these savings could not be made, it had already been told that it would have to identify other savings. Such savings, in turn, would mean 'reductions in community support services [which] may leave people with no option but to move into residential care'. The Director concluded by saying that although the proposal 'has not been "finance-driven" the Committee has to balance its budget in 1991/92 and beyond'.

Here the Director was clearly echoing the views of colleagues in other authorities; in their view it was impossible to examine home transfers other than in this context of continuing financial constraint. Given this context, it was said, authorities naturally responded as they did to the 'window of oppor-tunity' for revenue savings offered by the changing social security benefit arrangements. Moreover, the opportunity to create a more mixed economy of social care was largely incidental to the opportunity to take advantage of the available financial incentives.

8
Conclusions

The enabling role

This book has been concerned with the adoption of the enabling role by social services departments in the context of the fundamental changes to the funding and management of community care which were progressively introduced between 1991 and 1993. It has been based upon an analysis of the policy and institutional frameworks for those changes, together with evidence from fieldwork interviews conducted in a representative sample of social services authorities. The data from the latter source suggested an apparent contradiction: while all authorities accepted the legitimacy of adopting an enabling role in response to *Caring for People*, only a handful were fully supportive of the concept in the terms in which the authors of the White Paper had intended it to be understood.

We have previously noted that the concept of enabling has been subject to a process of evolution and substantial redefinition within the fields of local government generally and the personal social services more particularly. In addition, elements of somewhat different understandings of enabling could be identified within *Caring for People*. Perhaps most fundamentally, however, central government's policies for local government and its introduction of competitive forces into the supply of health and social care services rested on a definition of the enabling role which conflicted with other definitions originating in local government and social care. Moreover, the Directors and Chairs we interviewed attached different meanings and emphases to that role. We concluded, therefore, that the widespread consensus we found around the White Paper's central objectives and values (such as choice, independence, needs-led planning and enabling) derived from two sources: first, they were perceived as self-evident 'goods'; and, second, a number of those concepts – and especially that of enabling – could be invested with different meanings by different stakeholders in national and local policy networks. This latter conclusion explains the wide variations in the way in which Directors, Chairs and the Department of Health defined, understood and carried out their respective implementation tasks.

Thus, in order to understand authorities' responses to *Caring for People*, and the pace and direction of movement towards the enabling role, we need to be clear about who is being enabled, by whom and to what end. An analysis of the literature (see Chapter 2) and our interviews suggests three 'models' of enabling in respect of these questions: enabling as personal development; enabling as community development; and enabling as market development. While each implies different roles, tasks and emphases for social services departments, they should not be seen as either mutually exclusive or necessarily mutually reinforcing. Indeed, the second and third can be viewed, at least in part, as alternative means to achieving the ends specified in the first.

Enabling as personal development

At the heart of this approach is the enabling of individual users and carers to achieve improvements in their welfare and to participate in 'ordinary' lifestyles. It implies working to maximize the potential of individuals and to enable them to influence the design and delivery of services to secure that end. It also implies a commitment to develop services which not only enable carers to care but also enable them to share more fully in patterns of everyday living. This approach to enabling has been the driving force behind, for example, the All Wales Strategy (Welsh Office 1983), much of the Care in the Community demonstration programme (Knapp *et al.* 1992a) and the 'ordinary life' initiative (Towell 1988). It is, moreover, consistent with some of the most fundamental and enduring values of social work practice (Utting 1990). The underlying aims and objectives of *Caring for People* (see, for example, paras 1.8–1.11 and 2.1–2.2) strongly reflect this concept of enabling and, in this respect, the White Paper is clearly based on concepts of good practice which have emerged from the field in recent years (Wistow and Henwood 1991). From this perspective, indeed, *Caring for People* may be seen as both reflecting and legitimating practice-driven developments over the past decade rather than as providing the initial spur to such developments. It was, no doubt, largely because of this background that this version of the enabling role was generally recognized and supported by the authorities in this study.

Enabling as community development

In contrast with the previous emphasis on enabling and empowering individuals, this second 'model' has a stronger focus on collective action. It
contains two central elements. First, it stresses the mobilization and support
of community-based resources, especially those of the informal and local
voluntary sectors, in order to foster participation and democratize decision-
making. Second, it suggests a role for social services authorities based less on
the direct provision of their own services and more on shaping and influencing
the wider range of resources available within the communities they serve.
These elements are the essence of the enabling role as it first came to be
expressed in the personal social services. Their influence is readily apparent
in the Barclay report (1982), Norman Fowler's (1984) Buxton speech and
substantial elements of the Griffiths report (1988); although, as we noted in
Chapter 2, a different concept of enabling was also foreshadowed in the last
of these. In addition, they are consistent with the community social work
tradition which, although a minority influence within the social work pro-
fession, can be traced back to the Seebohm report (1968) and beyond. More
generally, Stewart (1986), Brooke (1989) and Clarke and Stewart (1990) have
developed similar concepts in relation to an enabling role for the local authority
as a whole.

Despite these antecedents, this version of enabling was largely eclipsed
in *Caring for People* by the new emphasis on contracting and creating markets.
It briefly recognized the importance of 'allowing scope for the emergence of
new, small-scale groups and to avoid the over predominance of large, well
established voluntary bodies' (para. 3.4.14). It also suggested that grant aid
remain an appropriate funding mechanism in some circumstances (*ibid.*). But
to a considerable extent, this concept of enabling was overtaken by the purchas-
er/provider framework and a 'contract culture'. The latter concept appeared
less acceptable than 'softer' notions of working with and alongside local groups
to enable them to develop their own services, albeit increasingly within a
framework of service agreements rather than general grant aid.

For a small number of our authorities, and especially Labour authorities
influenced by the wider concept of the enabling authority, it was this view
of enabling as community development that they have interpreted from the
White Paper and that provides the framework within which they are seeking
to diversify supply through the promotion of local and community-based
services. We discuss these authorities further on page 140, but they are to be
found within the two groups described in Chapter 6 as 'new beginners' and
'incrementalists'. They are represented by the authority whose mission statement began: 'Our purpose is to assure to the people of X a first class system
of information, advice, counselling, therapy and social and practical care for
socially vulnerable people and their carers.'

It was also because some authorities interpreted enabling in terms of
strengthening informal and neighbourhood care that they saw the inherent

fragility of such care systems as an obstacle to the creation of a mixed economy. It must also be said that the community development approach not only had the perceived advantage of being less associated with market values and mechanisms; it was seen by some authorities as offering the opportunity to protect at least a substantial core of publicly provided services by building up supply through local community organizations as an additional layer of provision rather than as a substitute for the public sector (see page 140). In this respect, therefore, it was an approach broadly consistent with the 'extended ladder' rather than the 'parallel bars' conception for the role of voluntary organizations (Webb and Webb 1912).

Enabling as market development

As we described in Chapter 2, the concept of the enabling authority outlined in *Caring for People* (paras 3.4.1–3.4.8) included three central elements: the separation, to at least some degree, of purchasing and providing functions within social services departments; the development and support of increased levels of activity by private and voluntary providers; and the regulation of provider agencies in all sectors (including the public sector) through procedures of service specification and contracting. It was recognized that alternative provider organizations were underdeveloped, especially outside the field of residential care. The role of social services departments was, therefore, to create as well as manage the mixed economy, a task which bore at least some superficial resemblance to the earlier tradition of enabling. Moreover, as indicated in Chapter 3, social services departments have always contracted out some services, including specialist child care provision, residential services and some specialized day care (for example, workshops for physically disabled people and the visually and aurally impaired).

None the less, as our discussion of enabling as community development implied, and the findings of our fieldwork confirmed, such activities are not to be confused with organizational arrangements based upon the creation of a distinct purchasing function and the promotion of competition between provider organizations. More fundamentally, the White Paper's description of the enabling authority represents the translation of the culture and values of 'the new public management' into the personal social services. Rhodes (1991), summarizing Hood (1991), describes the principal elements of this approach as compromising

> the following central doctrines: a focus on management, not policy, and on performance appraisal and efficiency; the disaggregation of public bureaucracies into agencies which deal with each other on a user-pay basis; the use of quasi-markets and contracting out to foster competition; cost cutting; and a style of management which emphasizes, among other things, output targets, limited-term contracts, monetary incentives and freedom to manage. (Rhodes 1991: 1)

That we categorized only three of our authorities as enthusiasts for market-making indicated the gulf between most social services departments and the kind of enabling role envisaged by the White Paper and reflected in many of the above 'doctrines'. That so many respondents, of all political persuasions, emphasized that social care is different in kind from other public services can be seen to raise questions about the limits of markets and/or the discrepancies between the traditional values and assumptions of social work and the personal social services, and those underpinning the 'new public management'.

That gap in cultures was also reflected in our interviewees' difficulty in responding to questions about their 'market strategies'. Indeed, the language and concepts of market creation figured rarely in our interviews. It cannot be emphasized too strongly, therefore, that whereas the first two versions of the enabling role are rooted in established concepts about what ought to comprise good practice in the personal social services, this third 'model' has no such roots, with the result that many members and officers questioned its compatibility with the values and nature of social care. However, it would be a mistake to imply that nothing had changed or was changing, in the management of social and community care. While we found concepts like competition, purchasing and market creation to have limited support in most of our authorities, there was equally little support for maintaining the status quo. In most authorities, however, the change agenda was conceived in terms of promoting and managing a mixed economy of care rather than in terms of competition and markets.

A more mixed and a more managed economy of care?

The term 'managing a mixed economy' implies diversity of supply and a purchasing function capable of specifying requirements in terms of identified need; together with systematic procedures through which an appropriate volume, mix and quality of supply can be purchased and monitored. It follows from our previous discussion that only a small minority of authorities were seeking to develop such comprehensive and coherent arrangements. However, some of their components were being developed by the majority of our respondents. We summarize our findings in relation to the purchasing and supply functions on the following pages.

Developing a purchasing function?

Mapping need and supply

At least a third of our sample had not yet decided how to map need, partly because they saw this as a priority for 1991–92 in producing their first community care plans by 1 April 1992. Few were attempting to link assessments by care managers with longer-term, authority-wide projections or community-based surveys of need. Most, however, were seeking to map need as fully as possible from a variety of extant sources. Perhaps inevitably, in this initial phase, much detail will be missing from these maps. A third of the sample were planning to develop joint information bases with district health authorities and/or family health services authorities. In addition, as indicated in Chapter 5, a number of authorities were seeking to involve users in need-identification processes through consultative and other mechanisms. Whatever the deficiencies of all these arrangements for mapping need, the requirement to produce a community care plan was prompting the assembly of data in a more systematic way than hitherto, and this process seemed likely to accelerate in subsequent years.

In addition, little work was being undertaken to develop the information base on supply. The diverse and changing population of voluntary organizations has presented perennial difficulties for statutory authorities seeking a detailed map of that sector. Some local authorities had commissioned intermediary bodies (for example, councils of voluntary service) to compile and maintain a register of local groups. But however comprehensive those registers in the localities where they existed, it was widely acknowledged that authorities' knowledge of the smaller-scale, less formally organized and possibly short-lived service providers was invariably incomplete or poor. Social services departments were no better informed about the private sector than about the voluntary sector. Thus, they were aware of the provision that they registered and inspected in the residential sector but they were rarely aware, certainly at headquarters level, of services which they were under no obligation to register. Moreover, even the registered private sector was, in some respects, more fragmented than the voluntary sector, frequently lacking the latter's intermediary and other umbrella groupings.

Linking purchasers with providers

There was considerable variation in the extent to which social services departments were developing linkages between themselves and providers in the non-statutory sectors. Only three departments had established a separate purchasing function and begun to draw up a comprehensive set of service specifications and contracts covering all services and sectors. At the same time, however, only two authorities (one Labour and one Conservative) fell into our category of 'conscientious objectors' who had rejected the case for tighter specifications and contracts. A further five (Labour) authorities had decided to introduce such procedures and nine more had concluded that they would expand them, albeit slowly. Most authorities had yet to decide on the type of tendering processes, and thus the degree of competition, they intended to introduce. However, the number of authorities favouring com- petitive tendering was small. The gradual evolution of service specification and contracting procedures was largely confined to relationships with the voluntary sector. This development was partly because the majority of authorities expressed a clear preference for working with traditional voluntary and new not-for-profit organizations – another reflection, in itself, of their doubts about the compatibility of markets with the provision of social care. Consequently, in 1991, relationships with private sector providers remained little changed and were primarily conducted through the traditional regulatory framework of registration and inspection.

Another factor limiting the formalization and extension of relationships (contractual or otherwise) with the private sector was the delay in implementing the social security changes. As a result, the immediate imperative to develop contracts with private residential and nursing homes had been removed. This factor may also have contributed to the absence in most authorities of a distinct purchasing function, a capacity which necessarily would have been developed by the time of our fieldwork in 1991 if the original implementation timetable had been maintained. At the same time, however, the phased implementation in principle allowed time for inspection units to become established and develop standards which could contribute to the specification process.

The diversification of supply

On the provider side of the mixed economy, two conclusions should immediately be highlighted. First, almost all the sample authorities emphasized the value of public sector provision. They were not uncritical, sometimes recognizing a tendency towards inflexibility and lack of responsiveness; but the majority felt that the public sector had provided good-quality services and should continue to do so. In effect, local pride was expressed in the defence of local public services. Second, however, many authorities were at least beginning to question whether the public sector could or should remain the provider of so comprehensive a range of services. This issue was sometimes raised *sotto voce* and with the acknowledgement that staff and other members of the committee or ruling group would not necessarily be prepared to address it at present. In a number of localities, however, budget-making was tending, if not towards market-making, then at least towards an implicit recognition that the gap between needs and resources could not be closed using existing services and service mixes.

It was not surprising, therefore, that in 1991 the most significant and substantial interest in diversifying supply surrounded the possibility of establishing not-for-profit trusts providing residential services and, less frequently, day care. Their significance was three-fold: first, they were resource-driven initiatives designed to generate income by shunting costs to the social security system and/or to obtain new sources of capital through the Housing Corporation; second, they were generally the subject of negotiations with a single supplier; and third, if successfully established, they implied a substantial reduction in the social services department's role as a direct provider, even though they were designed to enable the local authority to retain considerable influence over the services so divested. Even so, such arrangements would not, at least in the short term, generally lead to greater choice or variety in services; nor indeed were they designed with such objectives in mind.

Beside these initiatives, many of which had become becalmed in the wake of the announcement early in 1991 that the Department of Health was preparing guidance on their legality, the diversification of supply was limited. There was a tendency for it to be conceived as augmenting public sector provision rather than substituting for it, at least in the short term. Some existing non-statutory services, which had been established in the latter mode, were being brought into, or were potentially subject to, a new and more precise regime of specification and service agreements. In the case of new developments, the tendency was to encourage those where the department's services were not direct competitors.

One pattern beginning to emerge in a group of five (Labour) authorities was an interest in and/or the development of localized services provided by community and neighbourhood groups. This pattern clearly corresponded to the model of enabling as community development and, indeed, was encouraged with that objective in mind. Examples included services for ethnic minority groups and local luncheon clubs. Their purpose was not to replace extant statutory provision but to reach those parts it currently failed to reach. The longer-term consequences of their success, however, might be to undermine the viability of statutory services. One authority, for example, remarked on the lack of take up for its own luncheon clubs compared with those provided by community organizations. Such examples may be little more than straws in the wind for the present but they were significant for emerging in authorities which supported the Clarke and Stewart (1990) concept of an enabling role for the authority as a whole.

In general, therefore, we may conclude that a shift in what Vickers (1965) termed 'appreciative judgements' was beginning to take place in that the pre-eminence of statutory services was no longer assumed. A more mixed economy of supply was considered inevitable, although it was the residential sector (where resource incentives were mostly apparent and immediate) to which the divestment of provider functions was largely confined. Little was being done to promote the diversification of supply in the domiciliary services sector (only in one authority were non-statutory agencies being encouraged to provide such services on its behalf). However, it is important to remember that our fieldwork was conducted at only the beginning of the process of change initiated by the White Paper. In addition, the phased implementation of its provisions had taken some of the pressure off both the development of contracting and the diversification of supply. Moreover, the extent to which the economy of care is both mixed and managed reflects patterns of incentives which are not immutable, in themselves, but will be influenced by forces that implementation of the changes will progressively bring into play. Some of these incentives are identified on pages 144–6. First, however, we consider what is probably the most substantial shift to take place in the period during which the 1990 Act was implemented (1991–93): the recognition that social services departments were to become responsible for managing a market in social care.

Managing the social care market

During the latter part of 1991 and early 1992, the Department of Health began to give greater recognition to the nature and consequences of the market created by the switch of funding responsibilities from the social security system to local government. In effect, it began to acknowledge publicly that the implementation of the 1990 NHS and Community Care Act implied the creation of an external market in which there was real potential for disruption to the continuity of supply. Consequently, it began to pursue a risk management strategy based, in part, on the approach already adopted in its preparations for the introduction of the NHS internal market. There, too, the final year before implementation had been marked by the sudden appearance of an emphasis from the centre on 'no surprises', 'smooth take-off' and 'steady state'.

Perhaps significantly, the first public indication of such thinking in respect of the social care market came from Andrew Foster, Deputy Chief Executive of the NHS Management Executive. In evidence to the Health Committee in January 1992, he emphasized that 'it is equally important that we develop a steady state managed approach to the move towards this desirable objective [community care] as we have in the Health Service reforms' (House of Commons Health Committee 1992: 50). A few days later, the Chief Social Services Inspector, Herbert Laming (1992), followed up this statement with the first public reference to the need for a 'smooth transition' to the funding and management arrangements. The joint Foster/Laming letters of March and September 1992 put flesh on these aims with their twin emphases on local authorities seeing current patterns of social security expenditure as an 'implied commitment' for the first year of the reforms (see Chapter 2), together with instructions that neither health nor local authorities should make 'unilateral withdrawals' of services in the year preceding implementation of the social security changes (Department of Health 1992b, c).

The conditions under which the social security transfer was allocated to social services departments and could be spent by them were similarly designed to underpin the steady state/smooth transition objectives:

- the allocation formula was weighted according to existing levels of independent sector provision and thus favoured authorities where the supply of residential and nursing homes was relatively well developed;
- each of the four annual tranches of resources transferred from the Department of Social Security was ringfenced for twelve months to prevent immediate leakage into other areas of local government or social services spending;
- 85 per cent of the total transferred in the first year had to be spent on services provided by the independent sectors;

- residents in independent sector nursing and residential homes were to receive an additional 'residential allowance' of £45 per week (£50 in London) which was not available to residents in local authority homes and thus provided an incentive for local authorities to contract out such care rather than provide it directly;
- health and local authorities were required to reach agreements by 31 December 1992 on arrangements for hospital discharge, including the purchase of nursing home places;
- finally, and only weeks before the 1 April implementation deadline, the Community Care Support Force (1993a, b) published advice on contingency planning and risk management.

These measures show the Department of Health's concern to minimize the risk of rapid and major changes in market conditions by ensuring that the vast majority of the transferred resources would continue to be spent in ways which minimized disruption to independent sector providers, hospital throughput and existing residents. In focusing on a strategy of 'minimal turbulence' during the first year of the market, the Department was inevitably restricting the capacity of local authorities to begin altering the balance between institutional and other services. Such an emphasis on securing a process of managed change can be justified by the need to balance continuity of supply for existing users, uncertainty about the pattern of demand which individual needs assessment would produce and the underdevelopment of alternatives to institutional care, especially in the independent sector. However, it is essential that other than in the short term, supply systems evolve along the dimensions we identified in Chapter 2 (see Box 2.1) and do not become set in concrete. It should be acknowledged, however, that the arrangement of individually tailored packages of care in domestic settings is generally a more complex, demanding and time-consuming task than organizing placements in residential and nursing homes, especially where the pattern of supply favours the latter. When all these factors are set alongside the interests vested in the current pattern of supply, the importance of reinforcing incentives to diversify provision is re-emphasized. Otherwise, 'steady state' could tend towards at least some degree of permanence.

There are, however, two aspects of the way policy has evolved since we completed our fieldwork which are of particular significance to our interests in market management and the further development of a mixed economy of supply. First, the policy developments outlined above comprise an implementation strategy which favours planning over the free play of market forces and, indeed, the protection of commercial rather than public sector interests from exposure to such forces. It might be argued that, whereas the government has intervened in housing, education and health services to create and strengthen market forces, the pattern of interventions outlined above in the social care market is designed to mitigate the effects of such forces, at least in the short term. To some extent these differences in approach may be more apparent than real. The government could be seen as seeking to strengthen an internal, bounded market in the NHS case while being cautious in the largely external social care market, where the risks are greater and more difficult to manage.

In practice, however, the government has also preferred planning to market forces as a mechanism for addressing the perceived oversupply of acute beds in London, within the context of the more bounded internal market in the NHS. This approach was reflected in both its commissioning of the Tomlinson (1992) review and the Department of Health's (1993b) response to that report. The adoption of a similar approach to social care reflects the interplay of the same forces which became evident when the NHS changes were introduced: namely, a recognition that we are dealing here with political as well as economic markets in which the costs of failure include political as well as financial embarrassment (Wistow 1992b). The management of social care through local authorities rather than directly by central government, as in the case of the NHS, does allow ministers to distance themselves somewhat from responsibility for implementation and to diversify blame. Even so, political intervention in market management is an inevitable feature of the operation of publicly funded markets. In the first place, ministers are unlikely to be able to evade responsibility for allowing market failures and distortions and, second, the conventions of public accountability for expenditure patterns and outcomes will similarly exercise a continuing influence (*ibid.*).

A second general point may be drawn from our analysis of the steps taken by the Department of Health to pre-empt market failure. Its objective was essentially to forestall the possibility of market disruptions caused by the bankruptcy of individual homes, that is by business collapse on the supply side. Nor was the concern about this possibility without foundation: there was evidence that high interest rates and other cost increases were leading to unprecedented levels of closures, bankruptcies and repossessions during the second half of 1992 (Clode 1992). Some six months later, the Registered Nursing Homes Association told the Health Committee that,

> according to information we have received from banks and finance houses, 15 per cent of all care homes at the moment are in a parlous state; they are bankrupt, in receivership or have made voluntary or informal arrangements with their creditors. (House of Commons Health Committee 1993c: Q493)

Reductions in the scale of residential care implied by the White Paper could be expected only to exacerbate the pressures towards commercial failure. At the same time, however, it is important to recognize that the underlying concern here is with the potential failure of individual businesses in the market for residential and nursing home care rather than with market failure in the broader terms of our analysis in Chapter 6. At some point, of course, the volume of such individual failures could, in principle, lead to the collapse of the market itself, in particular localities or more generally. Measures to regulate and manage market conditions are justified, therefore, especially since the costs and distribution of supply had been influenced by the somewhat different market conditions created by the former social security arrangements. None the less, the focus of the Department of Health was on only one, somewhat limited, dimension of market failure compared with the more comprehensive analysis provided in Chapter 6.

The importance of that analysis is more fundamental than merely to identify potential sources of failure in the social care market. Rather, it also allows us to raise questions about whether markets are an appropriate mechanism for production and distribution in the field of social care. More specifically, it raises the issue of whether they can deliver the outcomes for users set out in *Caring for People* in terms of independence, choice, cost-effectiveness and innovation. In effect, the White Paper asserts that the market has clear advantages over traditional hierarchies in maximizing such values. Nowhere, however, is there published evidence from the government to suggest that the policy changes within the White Paper were founded upon an analysis of the respective strengths and weaknesses of different mechanisms for achieving such ends. Its driving force lay in ideology rather than policy analysis. In widely asserting that 'social care is different', however, our respondents were effectively challenging the assumptions on which the White Paper's definition of an enabling role had been based. In addition, in favouring enabling as community rather than market development, a smaller number of authorities were being no less ideologically driven in challenging the appropriateness of those assumptions. We do not seek to offer an opinion on the validity of either approach, although we do think it important both to raise and to address these more fundamental issues about whether and in what circumstances social care markets are more likely to succeed or fail to achieve the ends for which they have been introduced. Further research, which the Department of Health has commissioned from the Nuffield Institute and the Personal Social Services Research Unit, will enable us to begin to explore such issues. For the present, however, we would simply emphasize that the community care changes are a large-scale social experiment based upon limited piloting. While the outcomes of that experiment cannot be predicted with any degree of certainty, their consequences must be monitored in terms of the values and principles on which *Caring for People* was founded.

Incentives for further change

A number of barriers and opportunities affecting the pace and direction of the shift to a mixed economy were identified in Chapters 5 and 7. We need not rehearse them separately here except to note that the principal influences are associated with resources rather than philosophy, whether concerning the role of markets or the promotion of ordinary living. We now outline some possible influences which may tend to shift the existing balance of barriers and opportunities in ways that encourage the promotion of a more mixed economy of supply.

- Care management is potentially a most powerful engine for the diversification of supply. Its rationale is to enable a wider and more flexible range of services to be offered and packaged according to individual needs. How far it becomes such a driving force depends on the level to which budgets are decentralized and the degree of purchasing autonomy given to individual care managers (Davies and Challis 1986; Flynn and Common 1990; Wistow 1992a). However, as assessment and care management systems are progressively implemented and mature, so new 'bottom-up' pressures to diversify supply will be injected into a process which has currently been driven largely from the top.
- The social security changes which took effect in 1993 will necessarily reinforce trends to establish distinct purchasing functions and, most particularly, service specifications and contracts with voluntary and private sector providers of residential care. The extension of such arrangements to local authority services will be a logical if not inevitable consequence of such developments.
- As arm's-length inspection units become established, they will increase the pressure for explicitness of standards and service specification, as well as becoming additional sources of expertise in these functions.
- With the social security system no longer providing a safety valve or vehicle for cost shunting, resource pressures will further encourage social services departments to look for new mixes of services and providers.
- The absence of a level playing field in residential care after April 1993 preserves incentives for local authorities to divest themselves of residential provision, freeing resources to purchase residential care from nonstatutory providers (including those offering alternatives to traditional forms of institutional care) or to purchase new mixes of services and providers in the day and domiciliary sectors. The latter allows diversification of provision from residential facilities to encompass, for example, respite care, outreach work and a base for care management.
- The investment in management development and information systems will enable the new public management to establish a stronger foothold in the personal social services and lead to a shift from administration to management and from direct provision to internal cost centring and external contracting.
- Notwithstanding scepticism within social services committees about the relevance and appropriateness of markets for social care, political and managerial pressures at the centre of local authorities will reinforce the shift towards contracting.
- The community care planning process will strengthen the mapping of supply and the involvement of local groups in the design and provision of services.
- Opportunities for joint purchasing will emerge from the community care planning process which will require local authorities to develop purchasing arrangements compatible with those of the NHS.
- Central government will further encourage the purchaser–provider distinc-

tion in social services departments through the promotion of good practice examples and the monitoring of 'laggards'.

These influences are not expressed here as predictions but as an exercise in scenario building. It is not intended to suggest that they will all materialize or that they will be of equal weight in themselves or between different authorities. None the less, we believe that they represent feasible scenarios and could prove to be mutually reinforcing as different elements of the reforms become established.

What needs to be emphasized, however, is that few if any of these influences, individually or in combination, will necessarily lead to the outcomes that the government intends the mixed economy to secure: competition, choice, cost effectiveness and more fulfilling lifestyles for users and carers. For example, continuing or residual concerns about markets for social care could thwart attempts to encourage competition, and merely result in a shift in the locus of monopolistic supply from the local authority to a semi-independent trust or a single, fully independent non-statutory organization. We have also suggested above that market development is not the only style of enabling potentially capable of securing the objectives of competition, choice, efficiency or desirable user and carer outcomes.

Our findings suggest both the beginning of cultural change within the personal social services and also that some of the components of the White Paper's enabling model are beginning to be developed. They also suggest that it is far too early to judge the effectiveness of any of the enabling approaches in the delivery of the White Paper's objectives for users and carers. However, it is no less clear that unless those objectives are reinforced and form the basis for monitoring the mixed economy, the new framework is more likely to be driven by resource and process factors than by needs and outcomes.

Appendix: The research strategy

The research on which this book draws was commissioned by the Department of Health and conducted between 1990 and 1992. The study had two principal aims:

- to map the extent of the existing mixed economy; and
- to identify local authority attitudes to and plans for developing greater diversity of supply.

Research was conducted in a sample of local authorities, selected to be representative of all English social services departments along five dimensions:

- political control at May 1990;
- total expenditure on personal social services per level of population in 1987/88;
- percentage of total expenditure on personal social services going to services provided by voluntary organizations and registered private persons in 1987/88, this being the nearest the revenue outturn data come to measuring contracting-out;
- percentage of total expenditure on personal social services going to general contributions to voluntary organizations and registered private persons in 1987/88; and
- percentage of all places in residential accommodation for the elderly in the local authority area which were in voluntary and private homes in 1986/87.

We initially selected a sample of twenty-five authorities, although one was subsequently dropped when it proved impossible to arrange interviews to the mutual convenience of all concerned. (This was a hung council, and the three main political parties wished to be represented at the one interview meeting.) Three other authorities declined to take part and substitutes were found. These substitutes were chosen so as to preserve the overall and authority-type representativeness of the sample.

Interview format

Interviews were semi-structured and tape-recorded. Interviewees were sent a precis of the schedule and a description of the research project's aims prior to the interview. Directors and Chairs (or their respective designates) were usually interviewed separately. Taped interviews were transcribed verbatim. (The quotes from officers and members used in this book were all taken from these transcripts.) In all, more than sixty interviews were conducted. The shortest took thirty minutes, the longest more than two hours: the majority lasted approximately ninety minutes.

The *officer interviews* in the twenty-four authorities were conducted with the Director of Social Services alone (sixteen authorities), the Director and Deputy or Assistant Director together (two), the Deputy Director alone (one), the Director of Planning, Research or Development (three) or the Coordinator or Head of Community Care Services (two). In one authority we interviewed an Assistant Director as well as the Director in order to collect more detailed information about some aspects of the mixed economy. The *member interviews* were conducted with the Chair of Social Services alone (eighteen authorities), the Chair with the Director or other officer in attendance (four), a spokesperson for the largest party in an authority with a hung council, and the Deputy Chair in another authority. Supplementary interviews were conducted with representatives of national bodies across the various sectors, and with health authority (three), voluntary sector (four) and private sector (two) representatives in some local authority areas.

Interview schedules

The officer and member interviews covered similar ground, although we were obviously looking for different perspectives on each authority's plans and expectations. The topics covered in the local authority interviews are listed in Boxes A.1 and A.2.

Supplementary information

Authorities within the sample were also invited to send background information describing their plans or policies for community care. Following the interviews we obtained the most recent revenue outturn data from the Department of Health, with the prior approval of authorities.

Box A.1 Topics covered in officer interviews

Reactions to the government's proposals

The authority's proposals and local relations
- The authority's preparations for implementing the Act.
- The authority's priorities and main proposals for change.
- User and carer involvement in the implementation process.
- Inter-agency dimension of the implementation process.
- Responses of members, employees, local agencies, users and carers to the authority's proposals.
- Effects of phased implementation.
- Impact of Department of Health's guidance.

Roles and contributions of the non-statutory sectors
- Local role of non-statutory agencies.[a]
- Involvement of non-statutory agencies in service planning and delivery.[a]
- Systems for assessing current and future provision and demand.
- Nature and scale of local authority funding of non-statutory agencies, and anticipated changes.[a]

Shift to an 'enabling' role: creating a mixed economy
- Perception of potential role of non-statutory agencies.
- Strategies for managing and stimulating the market.
- Opportunities, obstacles and incentives in the development of an 'enabling role'.

Impact on social services departments: managing the mixed economy
- Organizational and personnel implications.
- Perception of the future role of the social services department.

Note:
[a]   Are there/will there be any differences according to: the nature of services (i.e. residential, domiciliary, day care); or client/ethnic groups; or agency (i.e. 'for-profit', 'not-for-profit'); or geographical area?

Box A.2   Topics covered in member interviews

Reactions to the government's proposals

The authority's proposals and local reactions
- The authority's preparations for implementing the Act.
- The authority's priorities and main proposals for change.
- User and carer involvement in the implementation process.
- Responses of members to the authority's proposals.
- Effects of phased implementation.

Roles and contributions of the non-statutory sectors
- Local role of non-statutory agencies.[a]
- Involvement of non-statutory agencies in service planning and delivery.[a]
- Funding of non-statutory agencies, and anticipated changes.[a]

Shift to an 'enabling' role: creating a mixed economy
- Perception of potential role of non-statutory agencies.
- Strategies for managing and stimulating the market.
- Opportunities, obstacles and incentives in the development of an 'enabling role'.

Impact on social services departments: managing the mixed economy
- Organizational and personnel implications.
- Perception of the future role of the social services department.

Note:

[a]   Are there/will there be any differences according to: the nature of services (i.e. residential, domiciliary, day care); or client/ethnic groups; or agency (i.e. 'for-profit', 'not-for-profit'); or geographical area?

References

ACC, NCVO and AMA (1981) *Working Together*, Bedford Square Press, London.

Allen, I. and Perkins, L. (1994) *The Future of Family Care for Older People*, HMSO/Policy Studies Institute, London.

Ascher, K. (1987) *The Politics of Privatisation*, Macmillan, London.

Association of Directors of Social Services (1988) *Community Care: Agenda for Action* – response to Sir Roy Griffiths' report, ADSS, London.

Association of Directors of Social Services (1991) *Arrangements to Transfer Local Authority Residential Care Homes: Draft Guidance to Secretary of State's Directions*, letter to Department of Health, 30 July.

Association of Metropolitan Authorities (1990) *Contracts for Social Care: The Local Authority View*, AMA, London.

Audit Commission (1986) *Making a Reality of Community Care*, HMSO, London.

Audit Commission (1987) *Competitiveness and Contracting Out of Local Authorities' Services*, Occasional Paper No. 3, HMSO, London.

Audit Commission (1988) *The Competitive Council*, Management Paper No. 1, HMSO, London.

Audit Commission (1992a) *Community Care: Managing the Cascade of Change*, HMSO, London.

Audit Commission (1992b) *The Community Revolution: Personal Social Services and Community Care*, HMSO, London.

Barclay, P.M. (1982) *Social Workers: Their Roles and Tasks*, National Institute for Social Work/Bedford Square Press, London.

Beecham, J.K., Knapp, M.R.J. and Fenyo, A. (1991) Costs, needs and outcomes, *Schizophrenia Bulletin*, 17(3), 427–39.

Bradshaw, J. (1988) Financing private care for the elderly, in S. Baldwin, G. Parker and R. Walker (eds) *Social Security and Community Care*, Avebury, Aldershot.

Brenton, M. (1985) *The Voluntary Sector in British Social Services*, Longman, Harlow.

Brooke, R. (1989) *Managing the Enabling Authority*, Longman, Harlow.

Brown, C. (1992) Taskforce to oversee care in community, *The Independent*, 4 July, 2.

Bulmer, M. (1987) *The Social Basis of Community Care*, Allen and Unwin, London.

Clarke, M. and Stewart, J.D. (1988) *The Enabling Council*, Local Government Training Board, Luton.

Clarke, M. and Stewart, J.D. (1990) *General Management in Local Government: Getting the Balance Right*, Longman, Harlow.

Clode, D. (1992) The profit speaks, *Community Care*, 17 September, 14–15.

Community Care Support Force (1993a) *Managing a Smooth Transition – Joint Contingency Planning*, Department of Health, London.

Community Care Support Force (1993b) *Resolution of Disputes*, Department of Health, London.

Davies, B.P. (1990) The 'trade and industry' metaphor and its relevance to the Griffiths Report, in B. Bytheway and A. Johnson (eds) *Welfare and the Ageing Experience*, Gower, Aldershot.

Davies, B.P. and Challis, D.J. (1986) *Matching Resources to Needs in Community Care*, Gower, Aldershot.

Day, P. and Klein, R. (1987) The regulation of nursing homes: a comparative perspective, *The Millbank Quarterly*, 65, 307–47.

DeHoog, R.H. (1985) Human service contracting: environmental, behavioural and organisational conditions, *Administration and Society*, 16, 427–54.

Department of the Environment (1991) *Local Government Review: The Internal Management of Local Authorities in England. A Consultation Paper*, Department of the Environment, London.

Department of Health (1989) *Kenneth Clarke's Statement to Parliament on the Future Arrangements for Community Care*, Press Release 89/298, Department of Health, London.

Department of Health (1990a) *Community Care in the Next Decade and Beyond: Policy Guidance*, HMSO, London.

Department of Health (1990b) *Implementing the Community Care Changes*, Social Services Chief Inspector's letter to Directors of Social Services, CI(90)3, Department of Health, London.

Department of Health (1991a) *Purchase of Service*, HMSO, London.

Department of Health (1991b) *Implementing Community Care: Purchaser, Commissioner and Private Roles*, HMSO, London.

Department of Health (1991c) *Community Care: Review of Residential Homes Provision and Transfers*, LAC(91)12, Department of Health, London.

Department of Health (1992a) *Community Care – Special Transitional Grant Conditions and Indicative Allocations*, LASSL(92)12 (amended), Department of Health, London.

Department of Health (1992b) *Implementing Caring for People*, EL(92)13/CI(92)10, Department of Health, London.

Department of Health (1992c) *Implementing Caring for People*, EL(92)65/CI(92)30, Department of Health, London.

Department of Health (1992d) *Implementation of Caring for People: Corporate Contracts*, Letter from Andrew Foster, Deputy Chief Executive to Regional General Managers, 7 February.

Department of Health (1992e) *National Assistance Act 1948 (Choice of Accommodation) Directions 1992*, LAC(92)27, Department of Health, London.

Department of Health (1993a) *NHS Trusts: Interim Conclusions and Proposals for Future Enquiries, The Government Response to the First Report from the Health Committee,* Session 1992–1993, Cm 2152, HMSO, London.

Department of Health (1993b) *Making London Better*, Department of Health, London.

Department of Health (1993c) *Community Care Plans (Consultation) Directions 1993,* 25 January, Department of Health, London.

Department of Health and Social Security (1981) *Report of a Study on Community Care,* HMSO, London.

Department of Health and Social Security (1984) *Health Service Development: Collaboration Between the NHS, Local Government and Voluntary Organisations,* HC(84)9/ LAC(84)8, Department of Health and Social Security, London.

Department of Health and Social Security (1986) *Sir Roy Griffiths to Review Community Care,* Press Release 86/410, Department of Health and Social Security, London.

DiMaggio, P. and Powell, W.W. (1983) The iron cage revisited: institutional isomorphism and collective rationality in organizational fields, *American Sociological Review,* 48, 147–60.

Dusansky, R. (1989) On the economics of institutional care of the elderly in the US, *Review of Economic Studies,* 56, 141–50.

Efficiency Unit (1988) *Improving Management in Government: The Next Steps,* HMSO, London.

Ernst & Whinney Management Consultants (1986) *Survey of Private and Voluntary Residential and Nursing Homes,* report to the Department of Health and Social Security, London.

Ferris, J.M. and Graddy, E. (1988) Production choices for local government services, *Journal of Urban Affairs,* 10, 273-289.

Ferris, J.M. and Graddy, E. (1989) Production costs, transaction costs, and local government contractor choice, mimeograph, School of Public Administration, University of Southern Califoria, Los Angeles.

Firth, J. (1987) *Public Support for Residential Care,* Joint Central and Local Government Working Party, Department of Health and Social Security, London.

Flynn, N. and Common, R. (1990) *Contracts for Community Care,* Caring for People Implementation Document, Department of Health, London.

Forder, J. and Knapp, M.R.J. (1993a) Social care markets: the voluntary sector and residential care for elderly people in England, in S. Saxon-Harrold and J. Kendall (eds) *Researching the Voluntary Sector: A National, Local and International Perspective,* Charities Aid Foundation, Tonbridge.

Forder, J. and Knapp, M.R.J. (1993b) Market shares, Discussion Paper in preparation, Personal Social Services Research Unit, University of Kent at Canterbury.

Fowler, N. (1984) *Speech to Joint Social Services Annual Conference,* 27 September, Buxton.

Griffiths, R. (1983) *Report of the NHS Management Enquiry,* Department of Health and Social Security, London.

Griffiths, R. (1988) *Community Care: Agenda for Action,* HMSO, London.

Gronbjerg, K.A. (1990) Managing nonprofit funding relations: case studies of six human service organizations, Proceedings of the Independent Sector Spring Forum, Independent Sector, Washington, DC.

Gutch, R. (1991) *Contracting In or Out? The Legal Context,* NCVO, London.

Gutch, R. (1992) *Contracting Lessons from the US*, NCVO, London.

Hansard (1993) *Written Answers Col. 334*, 18 February, HMSO, London.

Hansmann, H. (1980) The role of nonprofit enterprise, *Yale Law Journal*, 89, 835–901.

Hansmann, H. (1987) The effect of tax exemption and other factors on the market share of nonprofit versus for-profit firms, *National Tax Journal*, 40, 71–82.

Hansmann, H. (1989) The two nonprofit sectors: fee for service versus donative organisations, in V.A. Hodgkinson, R.W. Lyman and Associates, *The Future of the Nonprofit Sector*, Jossey-Bass, San Francisco.

Hardy, B., Turrell, A., Webb, A. and Wistow, G. (1989) *Collaboration and Cost Effectiveness*, final report to Department of Health, Centre for Research in Social Policy, Loughborough University of Technology.

Harrison, S. (1991) Working the markets: purchaser/provider separation in English health care, *International Journal of Health Services*, 21(4), 625–35.

Harrison, S., Hunter, D.J., Pollitt, C.J. and Marnoch, G. (1990) *The Dynamics of British Health Policy*, Unwin Hyman, London.

Hatch, S. (1980) *Outside the State*, Croom Helm, London

Hatchett, W. (1990) Reading and waiting, *Community Care*, 20 July, 10.

Henwood, M., Jowell, T. and Wistow, G. (1991) *All Things Come (to Those who Wait?). Causes and Consequences of the Community Care Delays*, Briefing Paper 12, King's Fund Institute, London.

Hoggett, P. and Taylor, M. (1993) Quasi markets and the transformation of the independent sector, paper prepared for the conference on 'Quasi-markets: The Emerging Findings', School for Advanced Urban Studies, University of Bristol, March.

Hood, C. (1991) A public management for all seasons?, *Public Administration*, Spring, 1, 3–19.

House of Commons Health Committee (1992) *NHS Trusts: Minutes of Evidence, Wednesday, 22 January 1992*, Session 1991–92, HC198, HMSO, London.

House of Commons Health Committee (1993a) *Community Care: Funding from April 1993*, Third Report, Session 1992–93, HC309, HMSO, London.

House of Commons Health Committee (1993b) *Memorandum from the Department of Health on Public Expenditure on Health and Personal Social Services*, Session 1992–93, HC489, HMSO, London.

House of Commons Health Committee (1993c) *Community Care: Preparations for Implementation*, Fourth Report, Session 1992–93, HMSO, London.

House of Commons Social Security Committee (1991) *The Financing of Private Residential and Nursing Home Fees*, Fourth Report, Session 1990–91, HC421, HMSO, London.

House of Commons Social Services Committee (1985a) *Community Care*, Second Report, Session 1984–85, HC13, HMSO, London.

House of Commons Social Services Committee (1985b) *Public Expenditure on the Social Services 1984–85*, HC339, HMSO, London.

House of Commons Social Services Committee (1985c) *Community Care*, HCP–13–1, Session 1984–85, HMSO, London.

House of Commons Social Services Committee (1990) *Community Care: Funding for Local Authorities*, Third Report, Session 1989–90, HC277, HMSO, London.

Hoyes, L., Means, R. and Le Grand, J. (1991) Made to measure? Performance indicators, performance measurement and the reform of community care, unpublished paper, School for Advanced Urban Studies, University of Bristol.

Jack, R. (1990) Residual hearing, *Social Services Insight*, June, 5(12), 23–4.

James, E. and Rose-Ackerman, S. (1986) *The Nonprofit Enterprise in Market Economies*, Volume 9 of *Fundamentals of Pure and Applied Economics*, Harwood Academic Publishers, London.

Jenkins, K. (1992) Organisational design and development: the Civil Service in the 1980s, in C. Pollitt and S. Harrison (eds) *Handbook of Public Services Management*, Blackwell, Oxford.

Joskow, P. (1983) Reimbursement policy, cost containment and non-price competition, *Journal of Health Economics*, 2, 167–74.

Judge, K.F. and Knapp, M.R.J. (1985) Efficiency in the production of welfare: the public and private sectors compared, in R. Klein and M. O'Higgins (eds) *The Future of Welfare*, Basil Blackwell, Oxford.

Judge, K.F. and Smith, J. (1983) Purchase of service in England, *Social Service Review*, 57, 209–23.

Kavanagh, S., Schneider, J., Knapp, M.R.J., Beecham, J. and Netten, A. (1993) Elderly people with cognitive impairment: costing possible changes in the balance of care, *Health and Social Care in the Community*, 1, 69–80.

Kendall, J. (1991) A transaction costs overview of the role of the voluntary sector in the mixed economy of health and social care, *PSSRU Bulletin*, 8, 22–3.

Kendall, J. and Knapp, M.R.J. (1993) Definition of the voluntary sector, Johns Hopkins University, Institute for Policy Studies, Working Paper 5, Baltimore, Maryland.

Kendall, J. and Knapp, M.R.J. (1994) *The UK Voluntary Sector*, in preparation.

Knapp, M.R.J. (1984) *The Economics of Social Care*, Macmillan, London.

Knapp, M.R.J. (1986) The relative cost-effectiveness of public, voluntary and private providers of residential child care, in A.J. Culyer and B. Jönsson (eds) *Public and Private Health Services*, Blackwell, Oxford.

Knapp, M.R.J. (1987) Private children's homes: an analysis of fee variations and a comparison with public sector costs, *Policy and Politics*, 15(4), 221–34.

Knapp, M.R.J. (1989) Private and voluntary welfare, in M. McCarthy (ed.) *The New Politics of Welfare*, Macmillan, London.

Knapp, M.R.J. (1990) *Time is Money: The Cost of Volunteering in Britain Today*, Aves Lecture, Volunteer Centre UK, Berkhamsted.

Knapp, M.R.J., Beecham, J.K., Hallam, A. and Fenyo, A. (1993) The costs of community care for former long-stay psychiatric hospital patients, *Health and Social Care in the Community*, 1(4), 193–201.

Knapp, M., Cambridge, P., Thomason, C., Beecham, J., Allen, C. and Darton, R. (1992a) *Care in the Community: Challenge and Demonstration*, Ashgate, Aldershot.

Knapp, M.R.J. and Forder, J. (1993) Social care markets: forgotten lessons from the recent past, Discussion Paper 798, Personal Social Services Research Unit, University of Kent at Canterbury.

Knapp, M.R.J. and Kendall, J. (1991) Policy issues for the UK voluntary sector in the 1990s, *Annals of Public and Cooperative Economics*, 62(4), 711–31.

Knapp, M.R.J. and Missiakoulis, S. (1982) Inter-sectoral cost comparisons: day care for the elderly, *Journal of Social Policy*, 11(3), 335–54.

Knapp, M.R.J., Robertson, E. and Thomason, C. (1990) Public money, voluntary action: whose welfare? in H. Anheier and W. Seibel (eds) *The Third Sector: Comparative Studies of Nonprofit Organizations*, de Gruyter, Berlin.

Knapp, M.R.J. and Wistow, G. (1992) Joint commissioning for community care, Personal Social Services Research Unit, University of Kent at Canterbury, and

Nuffield Institute, University of Leeds. A shortened version was published as Knapp *et al.* (1992b).

Knapp, M.R.J. and Wistow, G. (1993) Market failure: commissioning success?, Personal Social Services Research Unit, University of Kent at Canterbury, and Nuffield Institute, University of Leeds.

Knapp, M.R.J., Wistow, G. and Jones, N. (1992b) Smart movers, *Health Service Journal*, 29 October, 28–30.

KPMG Management Consultants (1992) *Improving Independent Sector Involvement in Community Care Planning*, Report for the Department of Health, London.

Kramer, R.M. (1981) *Voluntary Agencies in the Welfare State*, University of California Press, Berkeley.

Kramer, R.M. (1988) Trends in contracting for the personal social services, unpublished paper, School of Social Welfare, University of California, Berkeley.

Kramer, R.M. (1990) Change and continuity in British voluntary organisations, 1976 to 1988, *Voluntas*, 1, 33–60.

Kramer, R.M. and Grossman, B. (1987) Contracting for social services: process management and resource dependencies, *Social Service Review*, 61, 32–55.

Krashinsky, M. (1986) Transaction costs and a theory of the nonprofit organization, in S. Rose-Ackerman (ed.) *The Economics of Nonprofit Organizations*, Oxford University Press, Oxford and New York.

Labour Party (1992) *Better Community Care*, Labour Party, London.

Laming, H. (1992) Speech to the Care Management and Assessment Seminar, 27 January, Social Services Inspectorate, Department of Health, London.

Lawson, R. (1991) From public monopoly to maximum competition: one authority's approach, *PSSRU Bulletin*, 8, 6–7.

Le Grand, J. (1990) *Quasi-Markets and Social Policy*, Studies in Decentralisation and Quasi-Markets 1, School of Advanced Urban Studies, Bristol.

Le Grand, J. (1991) Quasi-markets and social policy, *The Economic Journal*, 101, 1256–67.

Lipsky, M. and Smith, S.R. (1989) Nonprofit organisations, government and the welfare state, *Political Science Quarterly*, 104, 626–48.

Lynn, P. and Davis Smith, J. (1991) *The 1991 National Survey of Voluntary Activity in the UK*, Volunteer Centre UK, Berkhamsted.

Mabbott, J. (1992) *Local Authority Funding for Voluntary Organisations*, NCVO, London.

McCarthy, M. (1989) Personal social services, in M. McCarthy (ed.) *The New Politics of Welfare*, Macmillan, Basingstoke.

Mawhinney, B. (1992) Speech to IHSM/ADSS Conference, 10 July, Department of Health, London.

Maynard, A. (1991) Developing the health care market, *Economic Journal*, 101, 1277–86.

Means, R. (1991) Performance indicators, performance measurement and community care 'on the ground', Working Paper 3, SAUS, University of Bristol.

Mencher, S. (1958) Financial relationships between voluntary and statutory bodies in the British social services, *Social Service Review*, 32, 138–51.

Metcalfe, L. and Richards, S. (1990) *Improving Public Management*, 2nd edn, Sage, London.

Mocroft, I. (1991) The survey of local authority payments to voluntary and charitable organisations, *Charity Trends 1991*, Charities Aid Foundation, Tonbridge.

National Audit Office (1987) *Community Care Developments*, Report by the Comptroller and Auditor General, HC108, HMSO, London.

National Council for Voluntary Organisations (1990) *Contracts for Care: Issues for Black and Ethnic Minority Voluntary Groups*, NCVO, London.

National Council for Voluntary Organisations (1991) Contract used to reverse funding cuts, *Contracting In or Out?* Autumn, 6, NCVO, London.

National Council for Voluntary Organisations (1992a) The Vatman cometh, *Contracting In or Out?* Spring, 8, NCVO, London.

National Council for Voluntary Organisations (1992b) *Local Authority Funding for Voluntary Bodies*, NCVO, London.

Nelson, P. (1970) Information and consumer behaviour, *Journal of Political Economy*, 78, 311–29.

Netten, A. (1993) Costs, prices and charges, in A. Netten and J. Beecham (eds) *Costing Community Care: Theory and Practice*, Ashgate, Aldershot.

Netten, A. and Davies, B.P. (1990) The social production of welfare and consumption of social services, *Journal of Public Policy*, 10(3), 331–47.

Niskanen, W.A. (1973) *Bureaucracy: Servant or Master?*, Institute for Economic Affairs, London.

Nyman, J.A. (1985) Prospective and cost-plus Medicaid reimbursement, excess Medicaid demand and the quality of nursing home care, *Journal of Health Economics*, 4, 237–59.

Nyman, J.A. (1988) Improving the quality of nursing home care: are adequacy- or incentive-based policies more effective?, *Medical Care*, 26, 1158–71.

Nyman, J.A. (1989) The private demand for nursing home care, *Journal of Health Economics*, 8, 209–31.

Nyman, J.A. (1990) The future of nursing home policy: should policy be based on an excess demand paradigm?, in L.F. Rossitter and R. Scheffler (eds) *Advances in Health Economics and Health Services Research*, Volume 11, JAI Press, Greenwich, Connecticut.

O'Brien, J. (1986) A guide to personal futures planning, in G.T. Bellamy and B. Wilcox (eds) *A Comprehensive Guide to the Activities Catalogue: An Alternative Curriculum for Youth and Adults with Severe Disabilities*, Paul H. Brookes, Baltimore, Maryland.

Parker, R. (1987) *Elderly and Residential Care: Australian Lessons for Britain*, Gower, Aldershot.

Qaiyoom, R. (1992) Contracting: a black perspective, *Contracting In or Out?*, Spring, 5, NCVO, London.

Rhodes, R.A.W. (1991) Introduction, *Public Administration*, Spring, 69 (1), 1–2.

Rhodes, R.A.W. (1992) Local government finance, in D. Marsh and R.A.W. Rhodes (eds) *Implementing Thatcherite Policies*, Open University Press, Buckingham.

Ridley, N. (1988) *The Local Right: Enabling not Providing*, Policy Study No. 92, Centre for Policy Studies, London.

Robinson, J.C. and Luft, H.S. (1985) The impact of hospital market structure on patient volume, average length of stay and the cost of care, *Journal of Health Economics*, 4, 333–56.

Salamon, L.M. (1987) Partners in public service: the scope and theory of government–nonprofit relations, in W.W. Powell (ed.) *The Nonprofit Sector: A Research Handbook*, Yale University Press, New Haven, Connecticut.

Scott-Whyte, S. (1985) *Supplementary Benefit and Residential Care*, Joint Central and Local Government Working Party, Department of Health and Social Security, London.

Secretaries of State (1989a) *Working for Patients,* Cm 555, HMSO, London.
Secretaries of State (1989b) *Caring for People: Community Care in the Next Decade and Beyond,* Cm 849, HMSO, London.
Seebohm, F. (1968) *Report of the Committee on Local Authority and Allied Social Services,* Cmnd 3703, HMSO, London.
Seibel, W. (1990) Government/third sector relationship in a comparative perspective: the cases of France and West Germany, *Voluntas,* 1(1), 42–61.
Shaw, A. (1993) Shifting sands: the place of volunteers in the health and personal social services, unpublished paper, Centre for Research in Social Policy, Loughborough University of Technology.
Social Services Inspectorate (1990) *Management Development: Guidance for Local Authority Social Services Departments,* Department of Health, London.
Social Services Inspectorate (1992) *Getting it Together: Strategies for Implementation,* Department of Health, London.
Stewart, J.D. (1974) *The Responsive Local Authority,* Charles Knight, London.
Stewart, J.D. (1986) *The New Management of Local Government,* Allen and Unwin, London.
Taylor-Gooby, P. and Lakeman, S. (1988) Back to the future: statutory sick pay, citizenship and social class, *Journal of Social Policy,* 17(1), 23–39.
Titmuss, R.M. (1968) *Commitment to Welfare,* Allen and Unwin, London.
Tomlinson, B. (1992) *Report of the Enquiry into London's Health Service, Medical Education and Research,* HMSO, London.
Towell, D. (1988) *An Ordinary Life in Practice,* King's Fund, London.
Turrell, A. (1991) Consensus, Collaboration and Community Care for Elderly People, Unpublished PhD thesis, Loughborough University of Technology.
UKHCA (1993) *Submission to the House of Commons Select Committee on Health From the United Kingdom Homecare Association,* UKHCA, London.
Utting, W. (1990) *The State of Social Work,* The Third British Association of Social Workers Trust, British Association of Social Work, Birmingham.
Vickers, Sir G. (1965) *The Art of Judgement: A Study of Policymaking,* Penguin, London.
Vladeck, B. (1980) *Unloving Care: The Nursing Home Tragedy,* Basic Books, New York.
Walker, A. (1982) The measuring and social division of community care, in A. Walker (ed.) *Community Care: the Family, the State and Social Policy,* Basil Blackwell and Martin Robertson, Oxford.
Walsh, K. (1989) Competition and service in local government, in J.D. Stewart and G. Stoker (eds) *The Future of Local Government,* Macmillan, London.
Warburton, J. and Morris, D. (1991) Charities and the contract culture, *The Conveyancer and Property Lawyer,* November/December, 419–31.
Webb, S. and Webb, B. (1912) *The Prevention of Destitution,* Longmans Green, London.
Webb, A. and Wistow, G. (1982) The personal social services: incrementalism, expediency or systematic social planning?', in A. Walker (ed.) *Public Expenditure and Social Policy,* Heineman, London.
Weisbrod, B.A. (1977) *The Voluntary Nonprofit Sector,* D.C. Heath, Lexington, Massachusetts.
Weisbrod, B.A. (1989) The complexities of income generation for nonprofits, in V. Hodgkinson, R. Lyman and Associates, *The Future of the Nonprofit Sector,* Jossey-Bass, San Francisco.
Weisbrod, B.A. and Schlesinger, M. (1986) Public, private non-profit ownership and

the response to asymmetric information, in S. Rose-Ackerman (ed.) *The Economics of Nonprofit Institutions*, Oxford University Press, Oxford.

Welsh Office (1983) *All Wales Strategy for the Development of Services for Mentally Handicapped People*, Welsh Office, Cardiff.

Westland, P. (1988) Progress in partnership: a case study, in G. Wistow and T. Brooks (eds) *Joint Planning and Joint Management*, Royal Institute of Public Administration, London.

Williamson, O.E. (1975) *Markets and Hierarchies: Analysis and Antitrust Organization*, Free Press, New York.

Williamson, O.E. (1985) *The Economic Institutions of Capitalism*, New York, Free Press.

Wistow, G. (1983) Joint finance and community care: have the incentives worked? *Public Money*, 13(2), 33–7.

Wistow, G. (1987a) Increasing private provision of social care: implications for policy, in R. Lewis (ed.) *Care and Control: Personal Social Services and the Private Sector*, Discussion Paper 15, Policy Studies Institute, London.

Wistow, G. (1987b) Joint finance: providing a new balance of care and responsibilities in England? *International Journal of Social Psychiatry*, 33(2), 83–91.

Wistow, G. (1988) Health and local authority collaboration: lessons and prospects, in G. Wistow and T. Brooks (eds) *Joint Planning and Joint Management*, Royal Institute of Public Administration, London.

Wistow, G. (1990a) *Community Care Planning: A Review of Past Experience and Future Imperatives*, Caring for People Implementation Document CCI3, Department of Health and Social Security, London.

Wistow, G. (1990b) *Implementing Caring for People: Issues and Perspectives*, Paper Presented to the Association of Directors of Social Services, Annual Conference, 3 May, Blackpool.

Wistow, G. (1991) Inter-agency perspectives, in J. Morgan (ed.) *Community Care Futures: the Cliveden Debate*, KPMG Management Consultants, London. A revised version appears in Wistow (1993).

Wistow, G. (1992a) Organising for strategic management: the personal social services', in C. Pollitt and S. Harrison (eds) *Handbook of Public Services Management*, Blackwell, Oxford.

Wistow, G. (1992b) The National Health Service, in D. Marsh and R.A.W. Rhodes (eds) *Implementing Thatcherite Policies*, Open University Press, Buckingham.

Wistow, G. (1992c) Joint planning in a new policy context, *Health Services Management*, 88(1), 25–8.

Wistow, G. (1993) Inter-agency relationships: stability or continuing change?', in M. Titterton (ed.) *Caring for People in the Community: The New Welfare*, Jessica Kingsley, London.

Wistow, G. and Hardy, B. (1993) Linking needs and resources: the role of community care planning, in N. Malin (ed.) *Implementing Community Care*, Open University Press, Buckingham.

Wistow, G. and Henwood, M. (1988) Planning in a mixed economy: life after Griffiths, in R. Parry (ed.) *Privatisation*, Jessica Kingsley, London.

Wistow, G. and Henwood, M. (1991) Caring for People: elegant model or flawed design?, in N. Manning (ed.) *Social Policy Review 1990/91*, Longman, Harlow.

Wistow, G., Knapp, M.R.J., Hardy, B. and Allen, C. (1992) From providing to enabling: local authorities and the mixed economy of social care, *Public Administration*, 70(1), 25–45.

Wistow, G., Leedham, I. and Hardy, B. (1993) *A Preliminary Analysis of a Sample of English Community Care Plans*, Department of Health, London.
Wolfenden, Lord (1978) *The Future of Voluntary Organisations*, Croom Helm, London.
Wolfensberger, W. (1977) *The Principle of Normalisation in Human Services*, National Institute on Mental Retardation, Toronto.
Working Group on Joint Planning (1985) *Progress in Partnership*, Community Services Division, Department of Health and Social Security, London.

Name index

Subject index